Wife:

UNAFRAID

Renee Bollas

Numbers 13:30..."Let us go up at once and take possession, for we are well able to overcome it."

CONTENTS

Numbers 13:30..."Let us go up at once and take possession, for we are well able to overcome it."

CONTENTS

Esther 3:13-14 And the letters were sent by couriers into all the king's provinces, to destroy, to kill, and to annihilate all the Jews, both young and old, little children and women, in one day…A copy of the document was to be issued as law in every province, being published for all people, **that they should be ready** *for that day.*

It seemed evil would triumph. It was all but over. Bitter cries were heard all over the land.

Esther was not afraid.

Proverbs 31:21 She is not afraid of snow for her household, for all her household is clothed with scarlet.

In the face of fear, Esther stood up.

There was no panic. No cowering. No shrinking back.

Esther was ready. She was prepared.

Esther had a lifestyle of prayer and fasting.

Esther 4:16 "Go, gather all the Jews who are present in Shushan, and fast for me; neither eat nor drink for three days, night or day. My maids and I will fast likewise. And so I will go to the king, which is against the law; and if I perish, I perish!"

Esther knew she had to speak to her husband, the king. Wives have such influence on their husbands. While he may be one man, he impacts many others. She knew what she had to say, but she didn't run right in and blurt it all out.

Timing was everything.

She waited.

God had to speak to him first.

Esther fasted.

This word "fast" is the Arabic word "tsuwm." It's literal meaning is: 'to shut the mouth.'

There is a time and place for us to just shut up.

Even after her three day fast, she waited some more.

At the right time, Esther spoke.

God opened the eyes of her husband. He saw the deception of the enemy. The tables were turned on the enemy. His evil plot was defeated. A generation was saved.

Is it winter upon your soul? Are you fearful? Is your husband deceived? Caught in sin?

Fast and pray.

Fasting attaches us to the vine. It infuses us with power. Power we would not have otherwise.

John 15:5 I am the vine, you are the branches. He who abides in Me, and I in Him bears much fruit; for without me you can do nothing.

Fasting doesn't have to be for three days. Make it realistic for you personally. A few hours or skipping a meal is very powerful.

It made Esther brave.

Esther stood toe to toe with evil, even at the cost of her own life.

Acts 20:24 "But none of these things move me; nor do I count my life dear to myself, so that I may finish my race with joy, and the ministry which I received from the Lord Jesus, to testify to the gospel of the grace of God."

God fought for her. He won.

Esther prayed.

God intervened.

Stand in the gap for your husband.

Joshua 1:9 This is my command—be strong and courageous! Do not be afraid or discouraged. For the LORD your God is with you wherever you go.

Lord God, I pray for my husband. Open his eyes wide to see the enemies deception. Help me to keep my mouth shut so he can hear Your voice. Your voice is so much more powerful than mine. No matter what comes my way, I will not be moved. Help me to keep on praying. I will not fear. I will be strong and courageous against this great enemy. Make me brave Lord.

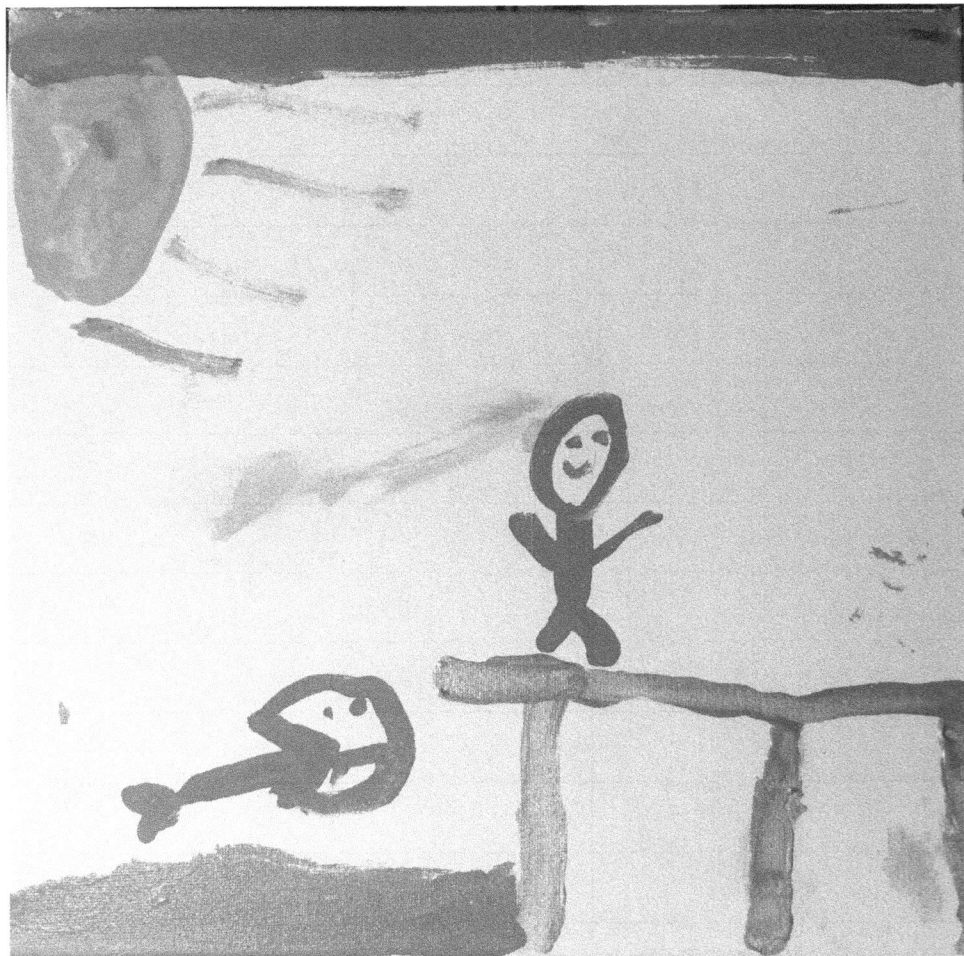

DAY 2
Trusting God's plan

The boys eyes were down, "This doesn't look like a masterpiece." He looked so disappointed. He hoped for something quite different. Sensational. Impressive. Beautiful. This wasn't what he wanted.

Marriage can be like that sometimes.

Completely opposite of what we hoped.

We see a big mess.

It doesn't look good.

In fact, it looks really bad.

How will this turn out? We want all the details. What? When? Where?

God doesn't always give us the details. When He doesn't, fear looms large.

Fear of the unknown can overwhelm an anxious soul.

Jeremiah 29:11 "For I know the plans I have for you," says the LORD. "They are plans for good and not for disaster, to give you a future and a hope."

God is creating a masterpiece with the canvas of our lives. Only He knows what the finished product looks like. He knows the plans He has for us. Beginning to end. We only see right here and now. And right now, it looks really bad.

Romans 8:28 And we know that all things work together for good to those who love God, to those who are the called according to His purpose.

All things? Yes, every last thing. Shameful things. Ugly parts. Difficult people. Hard to understand circumstances. He uses them all to fill in the canvas.

We can be tempted to take the paintbrush out of God's hand. Step in, and help Him out. Speed up the process.

Don't do it.

God isn't finished yet.

Be patient.

Works of art take time.

Father, You have good plans for me. Plans to prosper me and not harm me. Even though they don't look so good right now, I will trust you. You love me. I will not step out on my own. I choose to keep myself in your will. Help me to be patient as you finish your work in me and my husband. I ask you to paint a beautiful Masterpiece in my marriage.

DAY 3
"I'm gonna go to new heights!"

The boy got it right.

He wanted to go higher.

Higher than he's ever gone.

It took quite the effort.

What with stacking a stool on top of a flimsy plastic chair, one might wonder how he made it without getting hurt.

But, he did it.

He figured it out.

Sometimes it's hard to leave low living.

We need to take some risks to climb to new heights.

The enemy keeps us low. Whispering lies. Like, "you'll never get out of this place, this will never change, that will never happen, you might fall, remember what happened last time?…"

And on and on he goes. If we allow him. That's our choice. We can stay low.

Or we can dare to believe God.

This will change when I want it to.

Isaiah 52:2 …Loose yourself from the bonds of your neck, O captive daughter of Zion!

You cannot go anywhere with a chain around your neck. Chained to fear. Low expectations. Insecurity. Anxiety. Chained to the past. The lie that says, "This is the way it's always been. This is the way it will always be."

Dare to be believe God.

Loose yourself. Set yourself free. Take the chain off. You have to give it to Him. This is something you have to do. He can't do it for you.

Philippians 3:13 Brethren, I do not count myself to have apprehended; but one thing I do, forgetting those things which are behind and reaching forward to those things which are ahead…

We can't reach new heights if we're still holding onto the past.

Take that risk to love. Be willing to make yourself vulnerable. Yes, you may get hurt. It's worth the risk.

Put down your sword. Take off your armor of protection. You're on the same team.

Isaiah 52:1 ...Put on your strength...

Clothe yourself with Jesus, make no provisions for the flesh. Be determined. You don't have to live low anymore.

Jesus wants to take you to new heights!

Zechariah 4:6 Not by might, nor by power but by My Spirit.

Jesus overwhelm me with Your Spirit. I need your power to take me to new heights. I believe you can change me. I want change. Set me free from anxiety. I no longer want to be chained to my fears. I choose to trust You today. Every time doubts come to my mind, help me to relinquish them to You. Father, help me to open myself up to my husband. Take our marriage to new heights. I know we can soar for You.

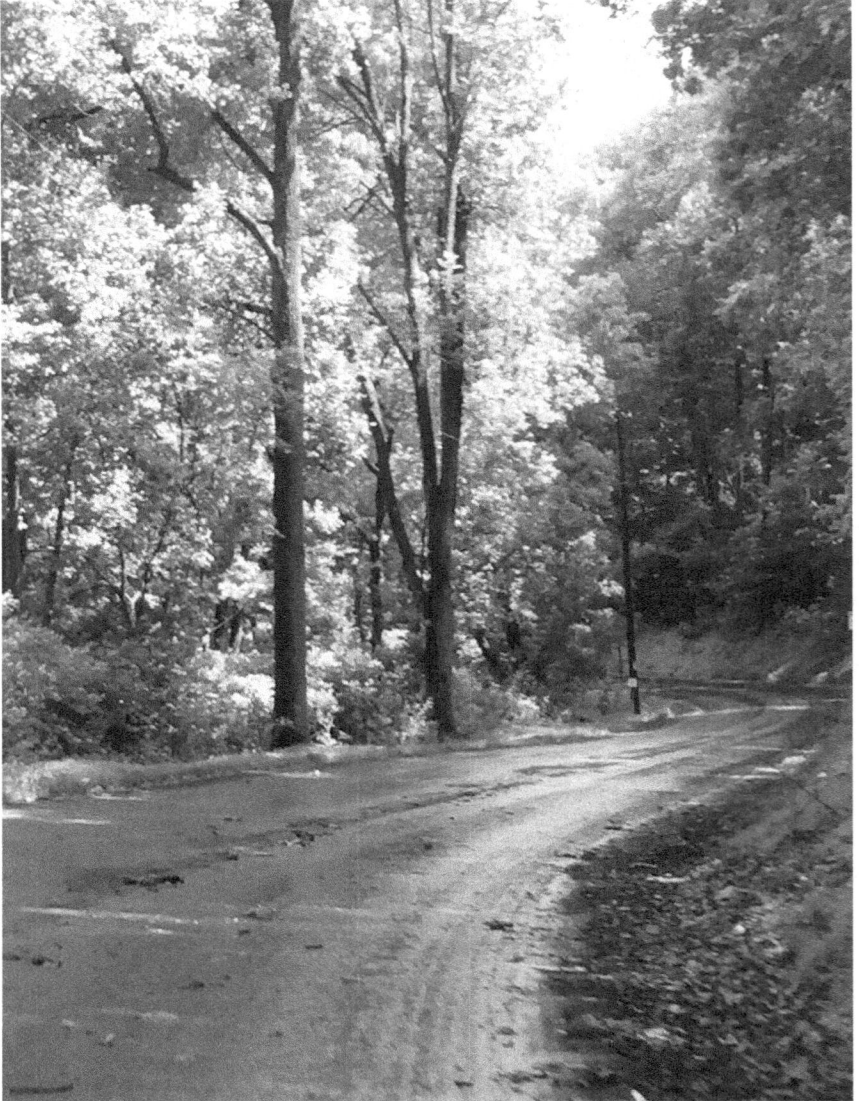

DAY 4
Our God is not slumbering

I pulled into the parking garage. It was dark in there. Much like my understanding that brisk morning. I really had no idea what to expect. But, the bigger unknown was the diagnosis.

What would these tests reveal? Would this turn out to be cancer? Could this be the beginning of a long debilitating illness?

I was scared.

Facing the unknown can be terrifying.

I heard this quiet voice in my heart:

Psalm 121:4 Behold, He who keeps Israel shall neither slumber nor sleep.

It spoke loud.

Instant tears were stinging my eyes.

The Presence of my Lord so tangible.

God was walking with me. Holding my hand each and every step of the way.

God is with you.

Our God is not slumbering. He never gets drowsy. He isn't lazy. Nor is He indifferent. He is an ever present help in our time of trouble. Now. In this moment. In this situation. Our God isn't sitting on the sidelines. No way. He is in the game. Actively involved in every decision.

Are there unknowns in your marriage?

Our help comes from the Lord; Maker of heaven and earth.

Romans 8:15 You did not receive the spirit of bondage again to fear, but you received the spirit of adoption by whom we cry out, "Abba Father."

We are not slaves to fear.

There is a war on for our minds.

Romans 7:23-25 But there is another power within me that is at war

with my mind. This power makes me a slave to the sin that is still within me. Oh, what a miserable person I am! Who will free me from this life that is dominated by sin and death? Thank God! The answer is in Jesus Christ our Lord. So you see how it is: In my mind I really want to obey God's law, but because of my sinful nature I am a slave to sin.

We must keep our minds fixed firmly on the Lord. It is a choice we must make moment by moment. Doing so will keep us at a distance from our problems and fears. He will take us higher and hold us up.

Psalm 33:16-20 The best-equipped army cannot save a king, nor is great strength enough to save a warrior. Don't count on your war-horse to give you victory—for all its strength, it cannot save you. But the Lord watches over those who fear him, those who rely on his unfailing love. He rescues them from death and keeps them alive in times of famine. We put our hope in the Lord. He is our help and our shield.

Lord Jesus, rescue our marriage from the plot of the enemy. Keep my mind fixed on you. Sustain us through this time of famine. Water the garden of my heart. Drench my soul with your Presence. Fill my husband with your Spirit. Make your Presence known and tangible to him. Feed our souls with your word. I rely solely on your unfailing love. My hope is in You Lord. Be my help and shield today.

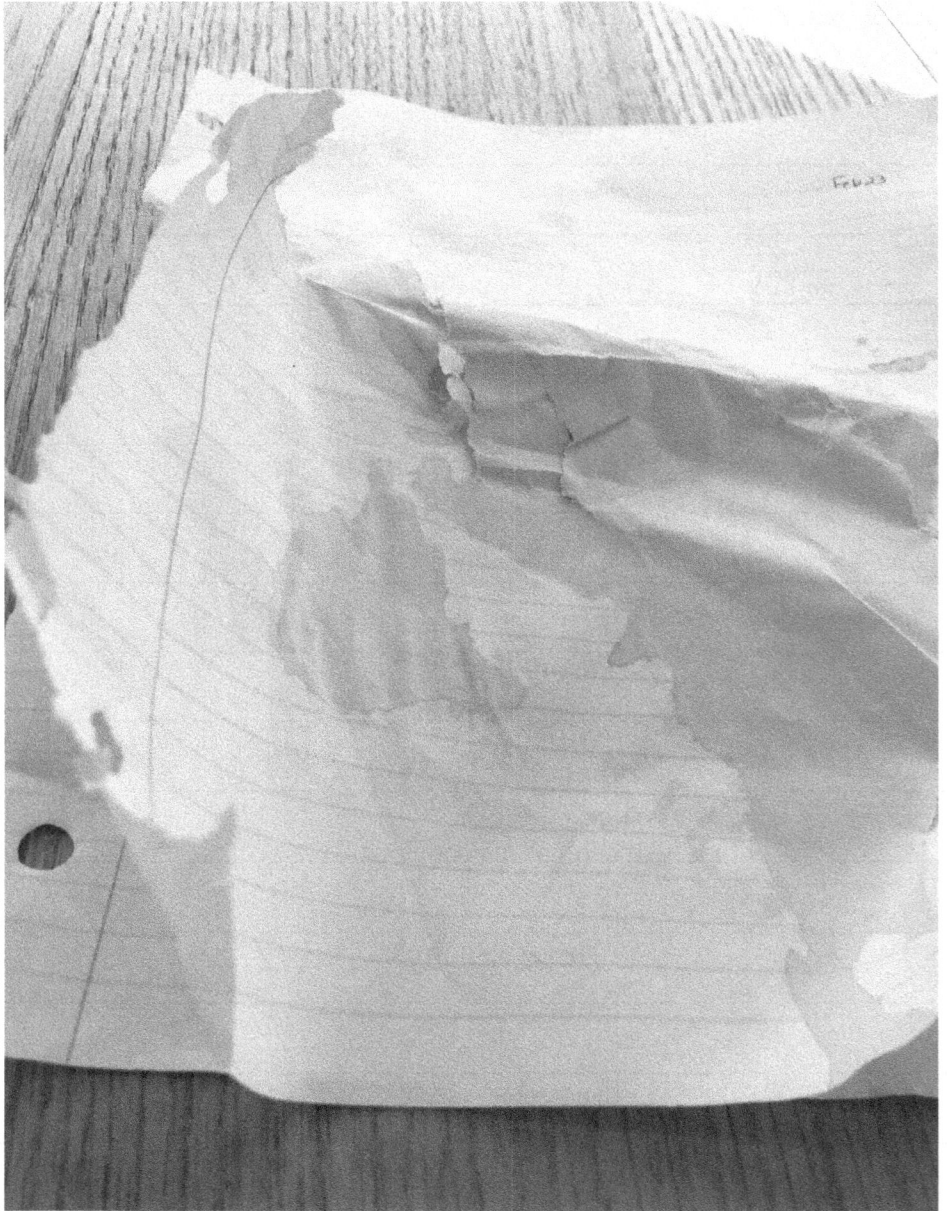

DAY 5
Embracing forgiveness

I can't believe I just did that.

That was so stupid.

As I sat down at my desk, I placed my coffee on my journal. A little groggy and not yet fully awake, I jostled the cup. Coffee spilled all over it. I sat there for a few seconds, immobilized.

Are you just gonna sit there and look at it, or are you gonna do something about it?

I had to do something about it. And quick. The longer it sat, the more damage it was doing. It already started seeping through to the next page.

I promptly went to the kitchen for some paper towels. As I tried to clean it up, the pages began to tear. I made the decision to just rip them out. They had to go.

Underneath? A clean slate.

No one would ever know that just moments ago coffee was all over the place. Threatening the whole notebook. A big ole mess. One that could've caused so much damage.

God's grace looks just like this.

Psalm 103:12 *As far as the east is from the west, so far has He removed our transgressions from us.*

Maybe you've done something foolish. Said something you shouldn't have said. Went where you know you shouldn't have gone. Don't keep going. If you do, it will seep through to every aspect of your life. Every relationship you have will be tainted. Especially your relationship with the Lord. It's impossible to live in sin and have peace in the presence of the Lord.

Stop.

When we come into agreement with God, yep, that was wrong, and we turn from it, and ask for forgiveness, He forgives.

Isaiah 1:18 *"Come now, and let us reason together," says the LORD,*

"Though your sins are like scarlet, they shall be as white as snow..."

That's an offer you can't refuse.

You can have a fresh start, a clean slate. A new beginning.

He rips that page out. He throws it into the depths of the sea.

He doesn't save it. He doesn't throw it back at us and remind us of it.

That's the gospel of grace. While we were still sinners, Christ died for us.

Perhaps your husband is in need of grace? If you're having a hard time forgiving him, it's helpful to remember how much you've been forgiven. Jesus doesn't measure sin. Size and extent are irrelevant. His blood was enough for it all.

For that, I am grateful.

Lord, I need you. Help me to forgive this man. You don't bring my sins up to me. I need your grace to bring a new slate into this marriage. Give me strength to put the past behind us. Separate this sin as far as the east is from the west. Love does not demand a change. It produces one. Let me be the first to change.

DAY 6
Be still and know

Are you feeling anxious?

Unrest in your spirit?

Turmoil within?

I was feeling just that way one morning. Trying to plow through my to do list. Decisions to make. Tasks to complete. Spinning my wheels and getting nowhere fast.

My mind was everywhere.

Why?

It wasn't as though I didn't spend time with the Lord. I did.

Why the unrest?

The Lord and I still had some unfinished business. He never answered me.

Let me rephrase.

I didn't wait for an answer.

Well, I was much too busy to just sit there.

I didn't have time for all that.

Turns out, I didn't have time not to.

Ruth 3:18 Then she said, "Sit still, my daughter, until you know how the matter will turn out; for the man will not rest until he has concluded the matter this day."

These words were spoken to Ruth.

Ruth went to Boaz. She shared her heart with him. Now it was up to him to conclude the matter.

He still needed to speak to someone else.

It was Ruth's job to sit still. Let Boaz do the talking.

Sitting still is often the hardest thing to do.

We like to do stuff. Fix things. Say more. Sometimes that can make matters worse.

When we go to the Lord with something, we can trust Him to do the talking.

Ten thousand of my words can't equal one word from the Lord. ~Pastor Tim Delena

1 Peter 3:1 Wives, likewise, be submissive to your own husbands, that even if some do not obey the word, they, without a word, may be won by the conduct of their wives...

Sometimes less is more.

This applies across the board. Not just with your husband. But, your co-workers. Your family. Your sisters.

Sometimes you've done all you can do. You've said all that you can say.

Now it's time to trust.

Proverbs 3:5-6 Trust in the LORD with all your heart, and lean not on your own understanding; In all your ways acknowledge Him, and He shall direct your paths.

God will speak.

Give him time.

Wait on Him.

Psalm 46:10...Be still and know I am God...

Lord God, I will be still. Speak to my husband. I've said all that I can say. Now I will allow you to speak. Help me to be quiet so he can hear You.

DAY 7
What's next?

"Mommy, I'm walking in your footsteps…"

That meant 3 things to me:

He was close. Real Close.

He could hear my voice.

And he could definitely see me.

It didn't matter that he wasn't sure where we were going.

We were together.

He could trust me.

Do you wonder what's next in your life?

Where should you go from here?

What should you do?

Psalm 143:8 Let the morning bring me word of your unfailing love, for I have put my trust in You. Show me the way I should go, for to you I entrust my life.

God loves you. He has a plan. If you are walking with Him, you won't get lost. You can't make a bad decision. His Spirit will prompt you anytime you're getting ready to do something out of His will. When that happens, stop.

When I don't know, I don't go.

Job 23:10 But he knows the way that I take; when he has tested me, I will come forth as gold.

Marriage brings many tests.

You may be walking a tough path right now.

God knows. He sees.

This is the hardest time to trust; when you don't know what's next. Here is what you do know:

You are God's precious daughter. He will not allow you to fall. If you must walk through trials and heartache, He will not leave you. He'll walk right through it with you.

You can trust God with your life.

Stay in step with Him.

John 10:27 My sheep hear My voice; I know them, and they follow Me.

If you can't hear Him right now, come a little closer.

Wait on Him.

Isaiah 40:31 But those who trust in the Lord will find new strength. They will soar high on wings like eagles. They will run and not grow weary. They will walk and not faint.

Jesus I know my marriage is being tested right now. I will trust you. Help me to not grow weary. I will walk closely by Your side. Fill me with new strength. Help me to endure. I am determined to please You. Speak to me Jesus, and I will follow.

DAY 8
Surrendering all

***Genesis 15:5,6,8** Then He brought him outside and said, "Look now toward heaven, and count the stars if you are able to number them." And He said to him, "So shall your descendants be." And he believed in the LORD, and He accounted it to him for righteousness. ... And he said, "Lord GOD, how shall I know...?"*

The Lord took Abram outside. He told him to look up at all the stars and gave him that wonderful promise: He would give him descendants that were as numerous as the stars in the sky.

That's a lot of stars. And that's a big promise to believe seeing that Abram had no children and his wife was barren. Abram believed. But we still know he asks God a legitimate question:

How?

God often confirmed His word with a sacrifice. Sacrifice often represents surrender. We don't always understand what God is doing or how He is going to do it. Sometimes it just doesn't make sense. God does desire for us to surrender our understanding.

***2 Corinthians 5:7** We walk by faith, not by sight.*

Has God asked you to believe Him for something big?

You need to live as though the thing that is not seen (the promise) is already visible.

Trust Him in a way you've never trusted before. Is He taking you way outside your comfort zone? Asking you to take a huge step of faith?

Step out onto nothing but His word.

Sometimes we do look at the situation and think it's impossible. We know it is.

***Luke 1:37** Nothing is impossible with God*

God tells Abram to bring Him a sacrifice: a heifer, goat, ram, dove, and pigeon.

He brought ALL the Lord asked. Have you brought ALL the Lord asked?

Full surrender?

Notice what happens when he brings all:

Genesis 15:11 Some vultures swooped down to eat the carcasses, but Abram drove them away.

This is exactly what happens to us when we grab hold of one of God's promises; the enemy swoops down to steal our trust. Steal our confidence. Steal our word. Steal our joy.

Has God given you a promise?

I am with you.

I will supply ALL your need.

I will change him/her.

I will intervene.

Don't let the "vultures" steal that word from you.

Keep in mind the vultures were the vessel. In our lives, the enemy will sometimes use our own family or friends to steal that word.

Drive them away. Right away.

In the Hebrew, the word for "drive away" often meant "to blow like a wind." It only takes one breath of the Holy Spirit to come drive the enemy away. One breath of the Holy Spirit to bring life. A single breath to raise the dead. Ask the Holy Spirit to come breathe on your situation. Drive out the voice of the enemy and allow the still small voice of the Lord to be louder.

Yes, the promise looked impossible. It was impossible.

NOTHING IS IMPOSSIBLE WITH GOD!!!!

He only asked Abram to believe. He didn't ask him to make it happen.

That's what the Lord asks of us. Believe. See the invisible. Believe the Promise.

The word of the Lord can be trusted!

Lord I believe You! Send the breath of your Holy Spirit to revive my faith. I see where the enemy has swooped in like a vulture to steal the promise You gave me. Drive the enemy away. Reaffirm Your word to me. Nothing is impossible with You God! Open the eyes of my heart to see You're working in this situation, even though I cannot see it outwardly.

DAY 9
Love even when it hurts

Exodus 36:12-13 Fifty loops he made on one curtain, and fifty loops he made on the edge of the curtain on the end of the second set; the loops held one curtain to another. And he made fifty clasps of gold, and coupled the curtains to one another with the clasps, that it might be one tabernacle.

What if one of these loops was missing? Or became detached? Or was ripped away? What if two were missing? Or three? There would be a gaping hole. The curtains certainly wouldn't be united and one, as God intended. Every loop is vital. These loops are a good semblance to the family of God. Each person is extremely important. Each one of us have a special job assigned to us. Unity is also a vital necessity in marriage. Without unity, we cannot do what God called us to do: Be His messengers. Be His hands and feet. Be His heart to a dying world.

When Jesus initially called His disciples together, He spoke about division.

Mark 3:23-25 So He called them to Himself and spoke to them in parables, "How can Satan drive out Satan? If a kingdom is divided split into factions and rebelling against itself, that kingdom cannot stand. And if a house is divided against itself, that house cannot stand.

Jesus desires us to be one with each other, one with our spouse, and one with our brothers and sisters.

Will disagreements happen? Fights occur? In the family of God?

Of course.

Jesus tells us very clearly what to do when we have an altercation:

Matthew 5:23-24...if you are presenting your offering at the altar, and while there you remember that your brother has something such as a grievance or legitimate complaint against you, leave your offering there at the altar and go. First make peace with your brother, and then come and present your offering.

Make peace. You go. Don't wait for him to come to you.

James 3:17-18 But the wisdom from above is first pure morally and spiritually undefiled, then peace-loving, courteous, considerate, gentle, reasonable and willing to listen, full of compassion and good fruits. It is unwavering, without self-righteous hypocrisy and self-serving guile. And the seed whose fruit is righteousness spiritual maturity is sown in peace by those who make peace by actively encouraging goodwill between individuals.

Do whatever it takes to love your man.

Jesus loved Judas to the end. The one who blatantly betrayed Him.

Matthew 5:44 But I say to you, love your enemies, bless those who curse you, do good to those who hate you, and pray for those who spitefully use you and persecute you.

Loving those we disagree with will take humility. There's no room for pride in the family of God, in our marriages, nor our ministries.

Pride takes many forms:

I must be right.

I must prove myself.

I must defend myself.

I must have my way.

I cannot be second.

Humility:

Is willing to do whatever it takes to reconcile.

Recognizes God's honor is at stake.

Covers others faults.

Trusts that the Lord sees.

Does not revile back.

Isaiah 53:7 He was oppressed and He was afflicted, yet He opened not His mouth; He was led as a lamb to the slaughter, and as a sheep before its shearers is silent, So He opened not His mouth.

God I want unity in my marriage. I will lay down my pride and go to him. I place all of my hurt at Your feet. Be my defender. I acknowledge I don't have a desire to be humble. Give me a willing heart. I need Your wisdom. Place in me a gentle spirit to do Your will.

DAY 10
Stay on the path

The warmth of summer was upon us. Kids laughter bubbled over. And the flowing water beckoned. It was right at the end of the footpath. A straight shot. No need to look for another way. Were there other ways? Of course. Each of them came with their own risks, unforeseen dangers and were downright life threatening.

This same truth is real in our personal lives.

Proverbs 14:12 There is a path before each person that seems right, but it ends in death.

No matter which way I "think" looks best, or would make me "feel" good, appears easier or appeals to me most, it may be wrong.

It may be wrong for me. May be perfectly fine for you, just not me.

How can I know what I should do?

Psalm 119:133 Guide my steps by your word, so I will not be overcome by evil.

This word "guide" in some places of scripture is used to describe an arrow. Our God will direct His arrows. He knows what He is aiming for. Many times we don't know or understand God's plan for our lives. This can be frustrating.

Isaiah 55:8-9 "My thoughts are nothing like your thoughts," says the LORD. "And my ways are far beyond anything you could imagine. For just as the heavens are higher than the earth, so my ways are higher than your ways and my thoughts higher than your thoughts."

God's word will show you what to do. He will make it clear. He will guide you. Maybe through Godly counsel or a Sunday message. He will speak to you.

Perhaps He already has?

Now all that's left to do is obey.

Ruth 2:8 Boaz went over and said to Ruth, "Listen, my daughter. Stay right here with us when you gather grain; don't go to any other fields. Stay right behind the young women working in my field."

Boaz was trying to protect Ruth from hidden dangers. That is what the Lord does for us. He wants to shelter us from things we know nothing about. He sees the big picture. We see here and now. That can be unsettling. People may not agree with us.

Psalm 119:42 Then I can answer those who taunt me, for I trust in Your word.

God's word is safe. It is a strong tower we can run to and be safe. It is trustworthy.

My feelings cannot be trusted.

I'll be perfectly candid. There have been times I've wanted to leave my husband. Run away and not come back. And I am sure he's felt the same. We've been tempted to give up. It would be much easier.

God's word superseded our feelings. God hates divorce. We had no grounds for it.

Never deviate from His word. If you do, it will be sure disaster.

I am so glad we stuck it out. God was making us stronger. Increasing our faith. Teaching us how to love each other unconditionally. Just like He loves us.

The kids stayed on that path. None of them got hurt. No poison ivy. And no snake bites.

It was the perfect day.

2 Samuel 22:31 As for God, His way is perfect; the word of the LORD is proven; He is a shield to all who trust in Him.

Lord I will trust in Your Word. My feelings deceive me. Your word is truth. I will cling to it with my whole being. Strengthen my marriage by the Power of Your Holy Spirit. As the enemy seeks to get a foothold, silence his devious lies. Quench all his fiery darts. I believe You are working in my husband. Reveal Your truth to both our hearts. You love our marriage. Your desire is to be glorified in and through it. Have Your way Father as I yield to You.

DAY 11
Willing to be vulnerable

He didn't run.

Me, I would've taken off quick.

It was a sure loss. Pain inevitable. Death a very real possibility.

Nope, that didn't matter. Odds were totally stacked against him. The enemy was coming like a flood; fast encroaching.

2 Samuel 23:11-12 And after him was Shammah the son of Agee the Hararite. The Philistines had gathered together into a troop where there was a piece of ground full of lentils. So the people fled from the Philistines. But he stationed himself in the middle of the field, defended it, and killed the Philistines. So the LORD brought about a great victory.

He put himself out there.

Shammah stood in a field of lentils. Lentils are not a tall crop. They are very small and low to the ground. There was nowhere to hide. Nothing to protect him from this mighty force coming against him. He was open and vulnerable.

The enemy attacked en masse. Brought all they had.

Shammah stayed. Everyone else ran away.

They called it quits. And who could blame them. They could see what was before them.

Certain defeat.

Are you ready to call it quits?

Have you reached your breaking point? After all, there's only so much a person can take.

We have our limits.

God wants to take us further. Stretch us. Grow our faith.

Will we stay and fight?

Shammah stayed. He didn't run away. He stood his ground.

He was willing to make himself vulnerable.

1 Corinthians 13:7...[love] endures all things.

He was open for attack. He risked his life. Staked it all on God.

He wasn't alone.

God fought the battle for him.

You are not alone in your battle.

Our great and mighty Savior is fighting for you. With you. And in you.

Even if it seems like too much to overcome. Stand and fight.

Jesus overcame death. There's nothing you can't overcome.

Don't give up. Pray. Your prayers are protection.

Fight for your man. Be willing to forgive. Ready to love.

Ephesians 3:20-21 Now to Him who is able to [carry out His purpose and] do superabundantly more than all that we dare ask or think [infinitely beyond our greatest prayers, hopes, or dreams], according to His power that is at work within us, to Him be the glory in the church and in Christ Jesus throughout all generations forever and ever. Amen.

Shammah stayed. He fought.

He won.

Lord, the battle is Yours and Yours alone. Fill me with the desire to stay and fight. I know You are with me. Give me the fortitude to stand my ground. When everything in me wants to run away, plant my feet firm in this marriage. You are living inside me. Fill me with courage to endure. I look to you for my victory.

DAY 12
Set free from our past

They weren't locked.

The handcuffs.

They were easy to open. All I had to do was push that little release button and they opened right up. It was very simple.

Freedom is that easy.

Sometimes we sit in these prison cells of our own making. Our thoughts. Chains of our own making. Bondage to fear. Handcuffed to the past. Sin. Regret. Failure.

Whatever it is that has a hold on you, bring it before the Lord.

Psalm 7:1 O Lord my God, in You I take refuge; Save [yasha: set free, open, rescue] me from all those who persecute me...

There is a voice that continually dogs us. It chases after us. Pursues and pursues. That's what this word persecute means in the old language. It means to pursue. Run after in order to catch. That's what the enemy does; he tries to wear us down in our minds until we give up. Don't give up!

There is freedom for the one who can grasp the fact that God knows all of her fears. He sees our hurt. Our Lord is well aware of our failings and sin. He knows us so completely; inside and out. When we are exhausted with our anxiety, He knows. He knows our desire to be understood, heard, seen, validated. Our need to be loved, and feel loved. Filled. Full. And healed.

Does something have possession of you? Today you can be free.

Ephesians 1:18-20 And I pray that the eyes of your heart the very center and core of your being may be enlightened flooded with light by the Holy Spirit, so that you will know and cherish the hope the divine guarantee, the confident expectation to which He has called you, the riches of His glorious inheritance in the saints God's people, and so that you will begin to know what the immeasurable and unlimited and surpassing greatness of His active, spiritual power is in us who believe. These are in accordance with the working of His mighty strength which He produced in Christ when He raised Him from the dead and seated Him at His own right hand in the heavenly

places...

The same power that rose Jesus Christ from the dead lives in us. It empowers us to overcome.

In His Presence we find freedom. His Presence brings refuge. The assault to our thought life is brought to a halt. Our thoughts of guilt, regret, discouragement, and hopelessness are deprived of power.

Proverbs 26:20 Where there is no wood the fire goes out.

Don't look at the past. Move on.

Philippians 3:13...I do not consider that I have made it my own yet; but one thing I do: forgetting what lies behind and reaching forward to what lies ahead...

Don't fear the future. Jesus is already there.

Combat the enemy with the word of God. Grab your sword. Jesus did. Shouldn't we?

Ephesians 6:17-18 Put on salvation as your helmet, and take the sword of the Spirit, which is the word of God. Pray in the Spirit at all times and on every occasion. Stay alert and be persistent in your prayers for all believers everywhere.

The enemy has no power over us; only what we give him. Give him nothing. Rather, give this "thing" to the Lord.

Luke 10:19 Look, I have given you authority over all the power of the enemy, and you can walk among snakes and scorpions and crush them. Nothing will injure you.

Authority: ability or strength with which one is endued.

Matthew 9:28 Do you believe I am able to do this?

Hit that release button. Take those handcuffs off. Be free.

Lord Jesus Christ, I have no power over this in and of myself. You have endued me with power to overcome. Crush the enemy. Take away my fears. Give me your peace that surpasses understanding. Guard my heart and mind. I believe you are able to do this. There are things holding my husband captive, set him free. I surrender him to You. He is Yours. I am being held captive in areas of my own heart. Set me free. Have the authority in this marriage.

Winter upon the soul

Spring was here. Warm days and sunny skies. Fluffy clouds beckoned a new season.

And then the snow came. Heavy.

The sheer weight of it threatened to break the branches of the trees. Since the bushes weren't expecting it, they too looked as though they would cave under the pressure.

Would it last long?

How much can one tree take?

Sometimes our hearts can feel like this. Disappointed. So weighed down, they may just break.

Psalm 69:15 Don't let the floods overwhelm me, or the deep waters swallow me, or the pit of death devour me.

Fear of the unknown can take us captive. Uncertainty of the future can bring us low and overcome our very being. It robs us of security. Steals our peace. Kills our joy.

Joshua 1:6 Be strong and confident and courageous...

Be strong in the Lord and the power of His might. Not your own power.

Be confident in the Lord. He will be with you. He will not abandon you. No. Never. He will be all that He says He is. Faithful. Trustworthy. A rock. A fortress. Immovable. Firm.

And secure.

Be courageous. Be brave. Things may not look good right now. But, He will make them good.

He is good.

Ecclesiastes 3:11 He has made everything beautiful in its time.

Everything. He redeems everything.

Broken hearts. Foolish decisions. Cancer. Autism. All of it. He redeems it all.

Psalm 69:29-30 But I am poor and sorrowful; let Your salvation, O God, set me up on high. I will praise the name of God with a song, and will magnify Him with thanksgiving.

David's answer to the floodwater, the heaviness, the uncertainty?

Praise God with a song.

Praise takes us above the situation. It brings us inaccessibly high. Higher than our enemy.

When we can sing during the storm, the dark night, in the midst of deep sorrow, it honors God.

When we seek His face before His hand, we see Him high and lifted up. Higher than the difficulty before us. We magnify Him, and our problems become smaller. The more we worship Him, the greater He becomes in our field of vision. We remember, no man can stand against Him. What He has done in the past he can do again. I remember what He did in Paul's life. And David's. And mine. Somewhere in the midst of the praise, I get lost in Him. I'm not captive anymore. I'm not bound by my worries and my anxieties. I am free. I am not a prisoner of my circumstances. Joy is a choice. I can worship Him freely. I can choose to be thankful because he is good and I have a lot to be thankful for.

If you find yourself in that stuck place, get your praise on!

Grab yourself a verse. Pray it. Own it. Make it yours.

Hear Him: I AM with you. I will not leave you. I AM in this with you. This is just a season.

Spring will arrive. It always does.

Psalm 30:5 ...weeping may endure for a night, but joy comes in the morning.

Lord, this situation is threatening to break me. I feel so lost right now. I don't know what to do. I look to You. You made a way through the Red Sea. A road for them to walk on. A path in the depths. Make a way for us. You are our protector. Shield us Lord. Make our marriage as the garden of Eden. Pure. Refreshing. Innocent. Delightful. Intriguing. Beautiful.

DAY 14
Will You still praise Me?

Mom called. She always wants two things when she visits. Small milkshake. Small fries.

Do you wonder where the boy gets it from?

A little voice from the backseat piped in, "Could I get a milkshake and fries too?"

He knows my usual answer is an an emphatic, "No."

Today was different. I told him, "Yes. You can have a milkshake and fries too."

He gushed, "You're the best Mudder in the whole world."

I felt a twinge of pain in my heart. I want him to think I'm the best mother in the whole world... even if I don't give him what he wants.

Immediately I heard the Lord's voice whisper soft, "If I don't give you what you want, will you still think I'm good? Even if I don't act in the way you think I should, will you still trust Me? If I say, "No" to your request, will you still praise Me?"

God doesn't always do what we think He should. We don't always get the result we're asking for. He doesn't always heal. He doesn't always act in the time frame I have set. We can feel the pressure.

Our fears can take over.

Joshua 1:9 "This is my command—be strong and courageous! Do not be afraid or discouraged. For the LORD your God is with you wherever you go."

Joshua was a leader. He was still afraid. If he wasn't, God wouldn't have said, "Don't be afraid." In fact, He didn't say it just once. He said it 4 times in one chapter.

Don't be afraid. I am with you.

Fears do come.

Fear says:

I can't... I won't... I'll never...

Faith says:

I can… I will… I must…

When fears come what should we do?

Have courage.

Courage is a state of mind.

That's where faith comes on the scene.

Hebrews 11:1 Faith is being sure of what we hope for and convinced of what we do not see.

We have many unknown variables.

But, we have a known God. A certain God. A God who fights for us. A God who is mighty. Strong. Powerful. A God who raises the dead. He can make the blind see, the deaf hear and open doors no man can shut. A good good God who always has our best interest in mind.

Philippians 4:8 Finally, brethren, whatever things are true, whatever things are noble, whatever things are just, whatever things are pure, whatever things are lovely, whatever things are of good report, if there is any virtue and if there is anything praiseworthy—meditate on these things.

Meditate on these things. Things that are true. Every word of God is true. Every word contrary to His word is a lie. Lies come from the thief who wants to steal. Dismiss the lies.

Whatever has come your way, you can know God wants to use it. He wants to reveal something about Himself to you. And others. Ask Him how you can use this to bring Him glory.

Romans 8:28 And we know that all things work together for good to those who love God, to those who are the called according to His purpose.

All things. Even things that don't look so good right now.

God, You are a good good God. You have always been there for me and You always will. Even if You don't do what I ask, I will still praise You. You are worthy of praise. Even if this goes the opposite way that I have planned, I will exalt Your name. Grant me a strong mind to stay in the battle. Until the end. Your honor is at stake.

DAY 15
Through the fog

On a good day you can see deep into the city of Baltimore. The view is vast.

This particular day was completely different. I was on the Francis Scott Key Bridge, I couldn't even see the end of the span. I really couldn't see much of anything. It was scary. I had to slow down. Way down. To barrel on ahead would be dangerous.

When life is foggy, it's good to slow down. Way down.

Sometimes that seems frustrating. We want to run ahead.

When in doubt, don't.

We hear that all the time. Why do we keep going? Sometimes it feels right. Our feelings are not good indicators. They deceive us.

Jeremiah 17:9 The heart is deceived above all things…

We want our way. Trying to force things to happen can only bring disaster.

When we're not sure, we can never go wrong by waiting.

You know the first thing I did when I entered the fog?

I immediately turned my lights on.

When we don't know where to go next, or what lies ahead, we can go to the sure thing. The Word of God. It never fails.

Psalm 119:105 The word is a lamp to my feet and a light to my path.

Align it up with the word of God.

God's word guides us.

Joel 2:32 Everyone who calls on the name of the Lord will be saved.

"My situation is urgent, and I cannot see how I will ever be delivered. Yet this is not my concern, for He who made the promise will find a way to keep it. My part is simply to obey His commands, not to direct His way. I am His servant, not His advisor. I call upon Him and He will deliver me."

~Charles Spurgeon

If you're in a foggy situation, slow down. Wait. Give God time to speak.

Psalm 27:13-14 I would have lost heart, unless I had believed that I would see the goodness of the LORD In the land of the living. Wait on the LORD; be of good courage, and He shall strengthen your heart; wait, I say, on the LORD!

Jesus, my Lord, guide me in all of my decisions. I won't take one step without you. I can't see what lies ahead. In this darkness, I will trust You. I will call upon You Lord. You hear my cries and You will answer. Help me to be patient as I wait on You. Strengthen my heart in the waiting.

DAY 16
Treasures of darkness

All alone he was.

Oblivious to those black clouds. Darkness all around. There he sat. Content. Digging in the sand. Shovel full after shovel full. He just kept going. Mining for gold. Sure, there were good things to be found on the surface.

But underneath?

There was a treasure trove more to be discovered.

It is that way in our trials.

We are forced to sit alone sometimes.

If we sit long enough, we'll find we're not alone.

God is with us.

Sitting. Holding us together.

Job 12:22 He discovers deep things in the darkness.

If we will wait upon the Lord, we'll find deep things. Secret things. Things we wouldn't find in the light.

Darkness brings us close to the heart of God. Much closer than the light.

True intimacy with the Lord comes from the fellowship of suffering. Friendships are forged in the fires of life.

We only reveal our heart to those we trust.

It's the same with God.

Sad times are not lost times.

Hard seasons reap untold treasures. Priceless gifts from the heart of God.

Jeremiah 33:3 Ask me and I will tell you remarkable secrets you do not know about things to come.

Jeremiah was confined to a prison cell for a second time when this word came to him.

God was giving him a message for others.

Are you going through a dark night?

Matthew 10:27 "Whatever I tell you in the dark, speak in the light; and what you hear in the ear, preach on the housetops."

Darkness is the time to listen.

Slow down. Be still.

The songbird learns to sing in the dark. ~Oswald Chambers

God has a precious message for you.

This time is not wasted.

Jeremiah 29:13 And you will seek Me and find Me, when you search for Me with all your heart.

In time, God will have you share that message with someone else who is going through their own struggle.

Lord you know my heartache. You see all my tears. Speak to me that word from heaven that I so desperately need to hear. Redeem this time. Don't let me waste it. Surround me with your comfort. I need You.

DAY 17
Rejected by men

The boy.

He didn't know the value of what he held in his hand.

Had no idea where it came from. The things it went through to reach that shore.

The miles traveled.

He didn't know how many other hands picked it up and tossed it carelessly. Discarding it as worthless.

He couldn't see the intricate detail put into it by it's Creator.

Truly, one of a kind.

He had no idea how fragile it was either.

When he threw it down, it broke in a hundred pieces.

Maybe you're feeling a little like this sand dollar.

Cast aside. Rejected. Broken.

It's so painful.

God wants you to know He was rejected. He feels your pain. He understands.

1 Peter 2:4 Coming to Him as to a living stone, rejected indeed by men, but chosen by God and precious...

That rejection never changed His value.

He remained God's chosen, precious Son.

You are one of a kind. There is no one else in the whole world who is like you.

That is purposeful. From a purposeful Creator.

Not just your Creator but your Father. Your Dad. You are precious to Him.

God loves you.

Stop and really think about this for a moment. He doesn't just love the whole world, he loves you. Personally.

You were created for a purpose. Your purpose is to make His heart smile. You do that just by being you. His love isn't based on performance.

He doesn't work that way.

When people hurt us and leave us and cheat and lie and call us names, we can begin to assume that identity.

We label ourselves ugly, fat, worthless, stupid, unlovable.

Peel those labels off.

All of them are lies.

You are a treasure. Valuable. Important. Beautiful.

Place your value back in His hands.

Let Him take those broken pieces of your heart and make it whole again.

Psalm 147:3 He heals the brokenhearted and binds up their wounds.

Lord, you know all the broken places I've come from. Help me to see myself as You see me. Holy Spirit reveal to me my true value. Only through You can I fully understand my identity as Your daughter. I am precious to You.

DAY 18
No backup plan

I hear Him loud. And clear.

Definite.

I know what is being asked.

It's just that I don't know how I'm going to do it.

It's hard. Really hard.

Acts 27:32 Then the soldiers cut away the ropes that held the skiff (lifeboat) and let it fall and drift away.

Cutting away the lifeboat meant cutting away the backup plan.

Everything they were relying on for safety would be gone. Still, they cut it loose.

And the storm raged on. It didn't go away.

Nor did Jesus. He was there.

Jesus was the backup plan. They just needed to be all in. Not planning an escape route.

Proverbs 3:5-6 Trust in the Lord with all your heart; do not depend on your own understanding. Seek his will in all you do, and He will show you which path to take.

Maybe the Lord is asking you to do something real hard. And you may be like me, questioning.

How?

How am I going to do this?

1 John 4:4 Little children, ye are of God, and have overcome them: for greater is He that is in you, than he (Satan) that is in this world.

This Power that lives inside us enables us to do hard things.

Resurrection power. The power that rose Jesus Christ from the dead. The power that opens the eyes of the blind. The power that moves mountains. The power that overcame death.

That Power will sustain you. It will empower you.

One step at a time.

That's all He asks.

One step at a time.

When you take that step, you find power to take the next.

Look to the cross.

You can trust the Man who died for you. Lives for you. Is fighting for you. Who loves you.

There is no greater love.

John 15:13 No one has greater love nor stronger commitment than to lay down his own life for his friends.

He won't let you go.

Lord, I trust You with all my heart. I have no backup plan. You are all I have. You are all I need. I am all in. I will do what You ask of me. Fully surrendered to Your will. Even if everything falls apart, I know You will be there.

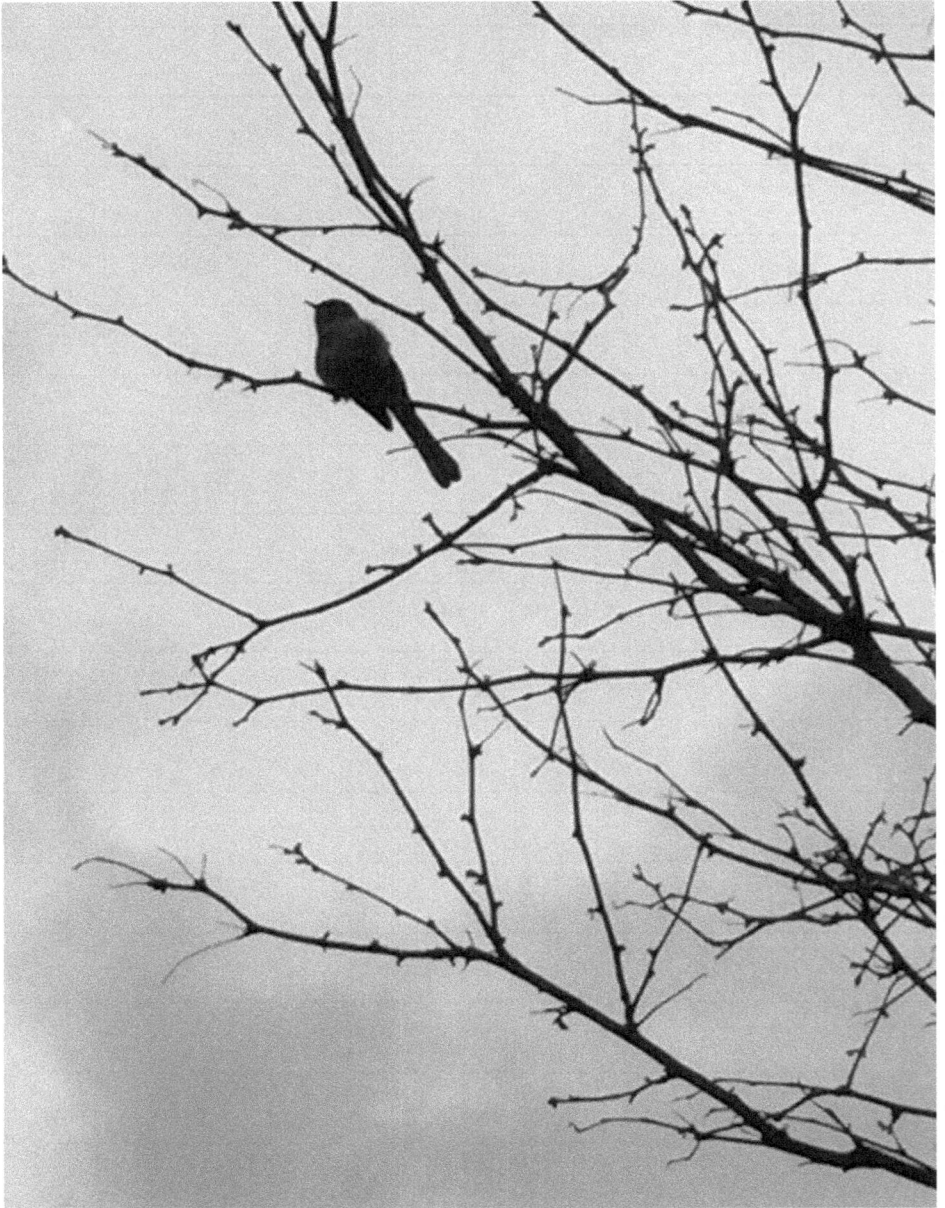

DAY 19
A new song

Are you despairing over a situation in your life?

Revelation 5:1-5 And I saw in the right hand of Him who sat on the throne a scroll written inside and on the back, sealed with seven seals. Then I saw a strong angel proclaiming with a loud voice, "Who is worthy to open the scroll and to loose its seals?" And no one in heaven or on the earth or under the earth was able to open the scroll, or to look at it. So I wept much, because no one was found worthy to open and read the scroll, or to look at it. "Stop weeping! Look, the Lion of the tribe of Judah, the heir to David's throne, has won the victory. He is worthy to open the scroll and its seven seals."

Jesus is holding the scroll of your life. He is in control of every detail. Beginning to end.

Keep your eyes fixed on Him.

Psalm 142:6 Hear my cry, for I am very low. Rescue me from my persecutors, for they are too strong for me.

The voice of the enemy chases after us continually. He dogs us. He aims to secure our thought life. He harasses us with discouragement. He lies to us. He says things will never change. This is hopeless. He causes us to look at others who haven't made it.

In the book "Pilgrims Progress," Christian and Hopeful end up in the dungeon of Giant Despair. On Friday, he tried to get them to kill themselves. On Saturday, angered that they hadn't, he showed them the bones of those murdered before them; assuring them this would be their fate as well. He beat them again.

At midnight, despite their wounds, they began to pray. They continued all night.

Then we read of the amazing escape: "Now a little before it was Day, good Christian, as one half amazed, brake out in this passionate speech; 'What a fool am I, thus to lie in a stinking dungeon, when I may as well walk at liberty? I have a key in my bosom, called Promise, that will I am persuaded will open any lock in Doubting-Castle.' Using the key, Christian and Hopeful escaped."

Sister, we hold the key to our dungeon. It's time to use it.

Our Promise is Jesus. He is our only way of escape.

Psalm 142:7 "Bring my soul out of prison, that I may praise Your name; the righteous shall surround me, for You shall deal bountifully with me."

Christian was beaten severely. His wounds were fresh. Still, he prayed. He prayed all night. A little before dawn, he escaped.

Your heart may have fresh wounds. Don't lie down in despair.

Acts 16:25 Around midnight Paul and Silas were praying and singing hymns to God, and the other prisoners were listening.

Rise up and pray. Sing to the Lord. Feel those chains of despair falling off.

Acts 16:26 Suddenly there was a great earthquake, so that the foundations of the prison were shaken; and immediately all the doors were opened and everyone's chains were loosed.

Jesus Christ commands your destiny. He holds the scroll of your life. Your marriage is in the hands of Jesus, not the enemy. Jesus is in full control, despite what it looks like.

Paul and Silas were free, but they stayed. They witnessed to their captor. He was saved; he and his whole house.

God uses our dark dungeon days. Even our chains of despondency.

Sing a new song to Him. Acknowledge that He is on the throne of your life. Your marriage. Your illness. Your depression. Your anxiety. Your loss.

Father, You are glorious. I am amazed by You. I ask you to surround me with songs of deliverance. Inhabit my praises. Take these chains of despair from me. Release me from the lies of the enemy that are holding me captive. Only You can restore what the enemy has stolen. This marriage is in Your hands. Hold us tight Lord.

DAY 20
Silence the mocking voice

Do you hear the mocking voice of the enemy?

You're not loved. You'll never do this. You're ugly. You're fat. You can't do that. You'll never overcome that. It's too big. Why are you wasting your time? Worthless. Stay in bed. Why try? He's gonna fail you...

And on and on. And on.

Elisha heard some mocking voices.

They were calling him names. Taunting him. Laughing. Scoffing. Making fun.

2 Kings 2:24 And he turned back, and looked on them, and cursed them in the name of the LORD. And there came forth two she bears out of the wood, and tare forty and two children of them.

I'm gonna challenge you:

Bring out the she bear in you!

Rise up with all your strength. Fight with all you've got. Silence these voices.

Hear the truth of God's word:

You are loved with an everlasting love. Jesus died for you. Not so that you could live a depressed, anxious, worried life, but to thrive. To be alive. Have joy. You are beautiful. A precious daughter of the King. Our Lord does not look at your outward appearance. He sees the heart. Your heart that beats for Him. Shines for Him. Wants to please Him. You will overcome. Because He overcame. He overcame death. That same power that rose Jesus Christ from the dead resides in you. Nothing you do for Him is ever a waste. It is precious to Him. He sees it all. Nothing goes unnoticed by Him. He who sees in secret will reward you openly. You are valuable. Your life is precious to Him. No matter what season you find yourself in, He has purpose for you. Jesus will always provide for you. You'll always have enough. Because He is enough to sustain you. He will never let you go.

Jesus never fails.

Now rouse yourself up.

Work double time.

The Lord has need of you.

Let's do this Lord! Today, I choose to listen to Your voice. Silence the voice of the mocker in my life. I am valuable. Worthy of love. Useful. You have appointed me to good works. I will rise up and walk in that truth. Produce a harvest in my marriage, ministry and life.

DAY 21
The battle is the Lord's

The boy got a bow and arrow. It was a gift. Naturally he wanted to do some target practice with it. Daddy bear was brave enough to put an apple on his head for the boy to shoot at. He missed the mark. Every. Time. He tried and tried. Aimed. Lined it up. Thought it out. Took his shot. But he stilled missed. Not for lack of trying. He made another attempt. Changed positions. Used a different strategy. Let the arrow fly.

Missed again.

He came close each time. But still missed.

Sounds like me. Me and all my efforts to "help" or "change" or "fix" my husband. All my pleading, exhorting, begging, coercion, and manipulating miss their mark.

I fail. Every. Single. Time.

I come up short. I go a little right. Try moving a little left. Say this. Say that. It gets so frustrating. That may be the understatement of the year. Maybe exasperating is a better word. And its beginning to show. My impatience and annoyance is written all over my face. It's stealing my joy. That's because I've taken on the Lord's job. That's a lot of pressure. Trying to run the world is exhausting.

"Our battles are won or lost in the secret places of our will in God's Presence, never in view of the world...nothing has power over the one who has fought the battle before God and won there...The reason the battle is lost is that I fight it first in the external world. Get alone with God, do battle before Him, settle the matter once and for all."~Oswald Chambers

I'm trying to do the fighting. I'm trying to do the changing.

The battle is the Lord's.

Isaiah 55:11 It is the same with my word. I send it out, and it always produces fruit. It will accomplish all I want it to, and it will prosper everywhere I send it.

God's arrows NEVER miss.

He is the expert marksman.

When we pray and ask Him to speak to that person, He will.

His word never returns void. It always accomplishes what it is sent to do.

I pray. He works. Not the other way around.

I decided to give Him back His bow. He's a way better shot than me.

Father, send that word that hits it's mark. You never miss Your target. Pelt this husband of mine with your piercing arrows that he will know it's You Lord. Your word changes us. It will accomplish what You sent it to do. Keep a guard on my mouth. Speak Lord.

DAY 22
In the presence of my enemies

Psalm 23:1-6 The Lord is my Shepherd [to feed, to guide and to shield me], I shall not want. He lets me lie down in green pastures; He leads me beside the still and quiet waters. He refreshes and restores my soul (life); He leads me in the paths of righteousness for His name's sake. Even though I walk through the [sunless] valley of the shadow of death, I fear no evil, for You are with me; Your rod [to protect] and Your staff [to guide], they comfort and console me. You prepare a table before me in the presence of my enemies. You have anointed and refreshed my head with oil; my cup overflows. Surely goodness and mercy and unfailing love shall follow me all the days of my life, and I shall dwell forever [throughout all my days] in the house and in the presence of the Lord.

Are you in the sunless valley?

Are you relentlessly pursued by the voice of the enemy?

His voice is subtle:

Quit.

Run.

Don't look back.

Hear the Shepherd's voice speaking gently:

I know all My sheep by name. I don't see My sheep as a large herd. I see them individually. I know your name. I know you inside and out. I am acutely aware of your hidden pain. The things no one sees. The heartache behind the smile. Your fears and they're so many sweet girl of Mine. Fear of failure. Fear of saying the wrong thing. Fear of not being enough. Fear of losing it all.

No one sees like Me.

Although I have you in a difficult valley, one you wouldn't choose, I'm walking with you.

I have gone before you. Clearing out the pitfalls. Anything that will hurt you. If a predator does attack, I'll be there. Through all of it. I won't leave you. All others may fail you, I never will. Don't quit. Don't run. Stay put.

I've prepared a special table for you and Me. A banquet table.

Will you join me?

It's an invitation I don't want to miss. I imagine the table set with the best linens. Fine china. Dainty tea cups. And a large mug for the Lord. Cinnamon chip scones and tasty treats abound.

Accepting, will be my highest form of trust.

Who can sit and sip tea surrounded by the enemy?

I can. And you can too.

Even though war may rise against you, the Lord invites you to rest at His table. Relax with the King. The Great Shepherd who is watching over you. Inviting you to come. Sit for awhile. He won't let you fall. Nothing touches you that He doesn't allow. He upholds you with His right hand.

Relax. Renew your strength. Abide with Him. Sing to Him as you sip tea together.

He has prepared a table for you in the presence of your enemy.

Join Him.

Lord in Your Presence is peace. I desperately need Your peace right now. Lead me through this sunless valley. Comfort me during this tumultuous time. My anxieties are real and they are many. None are hidden from You. Give me rest Lord. As I sit with You, I lay these hard things at Your feet. Take care of them. I need You. Fill me with Your Spirit.

DAY 23
Beady eyed fox

I see that little fox. Barely.

There he is again. It's almost like a blur. He's so fast.

It's always in the wee hours of the morning, just before sunrise, that's when I see him.

Little beady eyes peering over the hill at me.

In the cloak of darkness.

That's when the little foxes sneak in.

Song of Solomon 2:15 Catch all the foxes, those little foxes, before they ruin the vineyard of love, for the grapevines are blossoming!

They're never obvious. Just very subtle. Foxes are crafty. They are quick. Coming in and out before you even know it. They sneak off with your fruit.

Satan, that sly fox, works the same in our lives.

He comes in one unguarded thought.

That thing someone said to you will suddenly come to your mind. Or something someone did to you that you've long since gotten over, suddenly comes into your thought process.

You begin to dwell on it.

Before you know it, you've lost all your joy. You end up in the pit of despair; wondering how in the world you got there.

2 Corinthians 10:5 We destroy arguments and every lofty opinion raised against the knowledge of God, and take every thought captive to obey Christ...

Take these thoughts captive and cast them down. Away with you Satan!

Stay alert.

Recognize his plots, ploys and devices.

How?

John 15:9 As the Father has loved me, so have I loved you. Abide in

my love.

Abide in the love of Jesus.

Abide means to remain. To stay. Continue to be present. To last. And outlast.

Remain in a state of expectancy. Be all in. Even when it seems hopeless.

Satan wants to divide. He wants to divide you from the heart of Jesus. Divide you from your husband. He wants to sneak in and steal the promise God deposited in your heart.

Grasp hold of that promise and don't let go.

New things are blossoming. Satan hates that. Don't let him spoil what the Lord is doing in your life.

Trust unswervingly. Love lavishly.

Cling to the promise.

Lord Jesus guard my marriage from the crafty little foxes that sneak in undetected. I will dwell on You and Your goodness. Help me to take every thought captive and turn it over to You. Your Promises are true. You want to do something new in my marriage. I will stand on that promise. I will not be brought back into captivity of my fears. Your perfect love casts out fear. Empower me Jesus. Surround my husband this day. Give him eyes to see the ploys of the enemy. Protect him. Embolden him anew. Bless our marriage beyond what I think possible.

DAY 24
Stepping out in faith

1 Samuel 16:1-2 Now the LORD said to Samuel, "How long will you mourn for Saul, seeing I have rejected him from reigning over Israel? Fill your horn with oil, and go; I am sending you to Jesse the Bethlehemite. For I have provided Myself a king among his sons." And Samuel said, "How can I go? If Saul hears it, he will kill me." But the LORD said, "Take a heifer with you, and say, 'I have come to sacrifice to the LORD.'

Well, I hear Samuel. I feel his angst.

Lord, You're asking me to do something that's risky.

I might get hurt.

This may kill me.

Has the Lord called you to do something hard? Go somewhere? Step out in faith?

Do it as your offering to the Lord.

A sign of trust.

Samuel didn't trust Saul. He did trust the Lord.

Samuel did go.

The Lord said, "Fill your horn with oil, and go."

That flask of oil is symbolic of strength.

Go in the strength of the Holy Spirit.

You're not alone. I AM is with you. God has provided Himself.

Whenever the Lord calls us to do something difficult, He will always provide for us. He said it. He will do it. It may look impossible.

It may be risky. Even embarrassing.

Samuel didn't know what would happen next.

We need to obey step one first, then God will give us step two.

Stepping out into the unknown can be scary.

Don't be afraid.

You have the authority of Almighty God.

He will tell you what to do next.

Each. Step. Of. The. Way.

Baby steps. But, you must take step one.

Lord Jesus, You are asking difficult things from me. I will obey you no matter what the cost to me personally. My reputation is in your hands. I commit my heart to you. I know it may be broken again. Whatever You ask I will do it. I trust You wholeheartedly.

DAY 25
I've had enough

1 Kings 19:9-10 There he came to a cave, where he spent the night. But the LORD said to him, "What are you doing here, Elijah?" So he said, "I have been very zealous for the LORD God of hosts; for the children of Israel have forsaken Your covenant, torn down Your altars, and killed Your prophets with the sword. I alone am left; and they seek to take my life."

Elijah was beat down. I hear his heart:

I've had enough.

I can't take anymore.

I'm worn out.

The Lord heard his cries.

He spoke to him so gently, "What are you doing here?"

Elijah answered the question of why he was there. But that wasn't the question.

What are you doing here?

That was the question.

Elijah was hiding in a cave.

The Lord came and got him. He spoke softly.

1 Kings 19:11 Then He said, "Go out, and stand on the mountain before the LORD." And behold, the LORD passed by, and a great and strong wind tore into the mountains and broke the rocks in pieces before the LORD, but the LORD was not in the wind; and after the wind an earthquake, but the LORD was not in the earthquake; and after the earthquake a fire, but the LORD was not in the fire; and after the fire a still small voice.

The Lord comes and speaks to Elijah in that cave. Elijah was hiding. Doing nothing. He put himself out of commission.

That still small voice recommissioned him.

The Lord called him to come out of hiding. Get going. I have work for you to do.

If today finds you in a cave, hear the Lord's still small voice:

"I see you. I hear your heart. I know. Things have been too much for you. I am with you. You are not alone. I know you've been overwhelmed. I have a job for you. I need you to get up and get going. Come out of the cave. Reach out to someone today. Pray for them. Write them. Text them. Give them a smile. I love you. I am for you. You can do this."

Jesus, breathe Your breath of life upon me. Lift me up by the sheer power of Your word. Use me. I want to do Your will, O God. No matter what the cost is to me personally. I will do this for You. Give me the words to speak. Send me to that person who needs a word from Your heart. Help me to encourage and comfort them. Use me as Your hands and feet, especially to my husband. Give me your unending grace to serve this man you've given me.

DAY 26
"Mommy, is Jesus King?"

Mulling some tough things over one morning, these words fell like a gentle rain.

They came more as a reminder, not as a question.

They need to saturate my soul. Today. When everything feels like it's falling apart.

Is Jesus King?

Does He reign?

Is He on the throne of my life?

Revelation 1:8 "I am the Alpha and the Omega, the Beginning and the End," says the Lord, "who is and who was and who is to come, the Almighty."

The Almighty.

Almighty is made up of two Greek words, "krateo" which means "to hold" and "pas" meaning "all."

Jesus Christ is holding all things together for us.

Hebrews 1:3 who being the brightness of His glory and the express image of His person, and upholding all things by the word of His power, when He had by Himself purged our sins, sat down at the right hand of the Majesty on high…

He sat down.

Jesus is still seated on the throne of my life.

He was there at the beginning of my life. He will be there to the end.

Nothing catches Him off guard. I can let my guard down.

He is carrying my burdens. Bearing the weight.

Colossians 1:17 And He is before all things, and in Him all things consist.

Jesus Christ holds all things together in my life. Without Him, everything falls apart.

The Almighty. Omnipotent Jesus. The One who still holds sway over everything and everyone.

He is in control of every detail. Yeah, things may seem out of control.

Jesus is in perfect control.

Revelation 1:9 I, John, both your brother and companion in the tribulation and kingdom and patience of Jesus Christ, was on the island that is called Patmos for the word of God and for the testimony of Jesus Christ.

John found himself banished to the island of Patmos. It was a barren desert place. It was sweltering hot. He was suffering. A prisoner, yet free. It was during his captivity that he received the greatest revelation of Jesus Christ that one could ever hope for.

Our Father makes no mistakes.

If you will see Jesus on the island of Patmos with you, oh, the joy you will have.

The Almighty. Still has full authority. Strength. And power. He is holding all things together.

He is still seated. Even today.

Lord Jesus Christ, I exalt You. I lift Your Name high. You are sovereign over all. Even though things seem out of control, You remain in control. Seated and not threatened by the enemy, You reign. Hold me together today. Bear these burdens for me. They are too much for me to carry. Jesus, You are the King of my life.

DAY 27
Why's this happening?

Recently I went to a wedding. It was springtime, but it sure didn't feel like it.

It snowed.

I was hoping for sunny and warm. I got cold and dreary and dark.

Marriage can look like this sometimes.

Sometimes we're hoping for a new season. It doesn't come.

Or we hope to get out of a bad financial situation, only to find the hole getting deeper.

Maybe you are wondering, "Why is this happening?"

Psalm 139:23-24 Search me, O God, and know my heart; try me, and know my anxieties; and see if there is any wicked way in me, and lead me in the way everlasting.

Try me. Gold is tried best at high temperatures. It brings impurities to the surface so they may be skimmed off and thrown out. It's the only way to purify it. That's what the Lord wants to do in our trials. If you find yourself in a fiery trial, God wants to bring some things to the surface. Allow Him to remove them. He wants to purify you.

Look at the second half of these verses. In the Hebrew, the word "**wicked**" has a surprising meaning. It is used for the word "pain, sorrow or hardship." In some places of scripture it is used for the word "idol". Sometimes we can make our situations into an idol. Our pain or sorrow can become an idol. An idol is anything we think about more than God. So many times we go round and round thinking about this person or that situation. Over. And over. And over.

Instead, we need to think upon the Lord.

The Lord says, "I want you to trust Me. I want you to entrust this person or situation to me. I will provide for you. I am still the same. I want to change you. I want to put a new song in your heart through this. I want you to know, even in this situation, I am still God. Even if your situation doesn't change you can still sing. You can still praise Me. I will bring good out of it."

Philippians 4:19 And my God shall supply all your need according to His riches in glory by Christ Jesus.

He loves you. His heart is so for you. Trust Him.

Lord, I trust You. I recognize I am being tried right now. Show me the impurities of my own heart. I don't want to go my way. I want to go Your way. Remove anything in my heart that is not pleasing to You. I'm fixing my eyes on You. I will consciously choose to take my eyes off of this "idol" in my life. Lead me in Your way. Renew my mind Jesus. I don't want to constantly think upon the bad. I want to meditate on what is good. You are good.

DAY 28
Cheated on?

Have you ever been cheated on? Abandoned? Rejected? Unloved?

I certainly have. All those things can leave us feeling insecure. Less than. Worthless. Like our lives have no value. And no purpose.

The Word of God tells us something vastly different. Our self worth is found in Jesus.

John 1:4 In Him is life...

The word "life" in these verses is the Greek word "zoe." It means "absolute fullness of life. Life as God has intended it. Full of vitality. Fresh and vibrant."

If you're not living a fresh and vibrant life, you are missing out.

The Lord wants you to know your worth is only found in Him.

There's another word in that verse I want to point out. It is the Greek word "eimi". We lose it in translation. It means "I exist". My life exists only as it is found in Christ. Through His life. Our lives are hidden in Him. We live, move, and have our being only in Him.

Jesus Christ defines my life.

He defines your life.

You are loved with an everlasting love. A love that never fails. Your value does not lie in having or keeping a husband. Your value is found in WHOSE you are. You belong to Jesus. He loves you more than my words could ever say. Your worth is not found in the way people treat you or what they say about you, nor how many friends you have. You have a best friend in Jesus. He will never let you down. He'll always be there for you. He cherishes you. You are precious to Him. Because you are His. He made you perfect. Just. The. Way. You. Are. He loves you. Because you're you.

You are His treasure.

You are a daughter of the King of Kings and Lord of Lords.

Jesus gave His life for you.

Jesus wants you to find your value in Him.

Give Him your heart. Give Him your soul. Give Him everything and then you will have an absolute full life.

Jesus, I surrender these past hurts to you. I have allowed them to define me for way too long. I am Your daughter. You define me. I belong to You. My heart is Yours Lord. God, I ask You to heal all of these broken places in my heart. Give me my security back. Restore me fully and completely. I will only look to Your word for affirmation. Thank you for Your unfailing love.

DAY 29
Infiltrated enemy

Judges 5:31 "Thus let all Your enemies perish, O LORD! But let those who love Him be like the sun when it comes out in full strength." So the land had rest for forty years.

The enemy infiltrated. He was in Jael's tent.

But, she was ready.

She didn't waste any time. She quickly made an end of him. She took a tent peg and struck him through the temple.

Yeah, that was radical. This women was brave. I admire her courage. She took a big risk. Jael lived on the edge. She did what many women would be unwilling to do. We can learn a lot from her.

Has the enemy entered your "tent"? Your thought life? Your marriage?

Ephesians 6:12 For we do not wrestle against flesh and blood, but against principalities, against powers, against the rulers of the darkness of this age, against spiritual hosts of wickedness in the heavenly places.

Your battle is not with flesh and blood. The enemy is not your husband. Not your mother. Not your sister. Not your child. The enemy is Satan.

Ephesians 6:16 above all, taking the shield of faith with which you will be able to quench all the fiery darts of the wicked one.

God is faithful. So very faithful. Trust in Him. He is going to fully cover you with His protection.

Rely on Him. He won't fail you.

Your battle is spiritual. You need to fight with spiritual weapons.

Don't use your words. They will fall short.

Don't use manipulation. That won't work.

Don't try to play Holy Spirit. He does a better job…

You can grab your "tent peg" and crush the enemy.

Pray.

Ephesians 6:18 praying always with all prayer and supplication in the Spirit, being watchful to this end with all perseverance and supplication for all the saints—

Prayer is power. The Lord will give us power to recognize the enemy.

Here are just a few of mine:

Pride.

Ephesians 4:2 Always be humble and gentle. Be patient with each other, making allowance for each other's faults because of your love.

So many times a situation can be diffused by one person saying, "You're right. I am wrong." We want to press our point when yielding would be better. Even when we know the other person is wrong. The Lord will honor our humility.

Busyness.

Luke 10:42 But one thing is needful: and Mary hath chosen that good part, which shall not be taken away from her.

There are so many things pressing in on us. Vying for our attention. Push it all aside and sit at Jesus' feet. It's there you'll find what you're really looking for. Don't rush off.

Disunity.

Ephesians 4:3 endeavoring to keep the unity of the Spirit in the bond of peace.

Make haste for unity! Don't allow Satan an inch; he will steal a mile.

Come out against these enemies in full strength. Not your own strength, but in the strength of the Lord.

Ephesians 6:10 Finally: Be strong in the Lord and in his mighty power.

Lord, You are stronger than I am. I need You to overpower the enemy that has come out full force against my marriage, my husband and myself. Unify us. I cling to Your desire for us as a couple to love each other. I cherish this man you gave me. Overwhelm him with Your Almighty strength to be the man You called him to be.

DAY 30
Lost

I was lost.

Had no idea where I was.

I thought I did. I thought I knew where I was going.

This stretch of beach was long. It was unfamiliar.

I'd never been there before. I was just feeling my way around. I drifted off and lost my bearings.

There were landmarks to the house we were renting. A colorful kite tied to a wooden marker was on the dune directly in front of the house. A small for sale sign also sat direct center.

Still, I missed it.

Where was it?

I changed direction. I turned and went the other way. I just kept walking.

Still, I missed it.

Again, I changed direction. I walked some more.

Still, I missed it.

Now I was afraid.

I had no idea what to do.

Then it occurred to me; I'll call my friend. She's been here before. She'll lead me back to the house. She'll know exactly what to do. So that's what I did. Sure enough, she knew exactly where I was. She pointed me in the right direction and I was back safe and sound.

Proverbs 14:12 *There is a way that seems right to a man, but its end is the way of death.*

If you are uncertain which direction to go, stop. Call upon the Lord.

Why do we wait until we're desperate to call upon the Lord? We should call to Him first.

Acts 2:21 *...whoever calls on the name of the LORD shall be saved.*

When we call, He answers. Help is on the way.

He knows exactly where we are. He never loses sight of us.

Psalm 46:1 ...God is our refuge and strength, a very present help in trouble.

Lord Jesus, I need You now more than ever. I don't know which direction to go. I need your wisdom to show me the right way. Your way. Reveal Yourself to my husband so we can be on the same page. You hear me when I call. I know you will answer. Make your way clear to me. Until then, I wait on You.

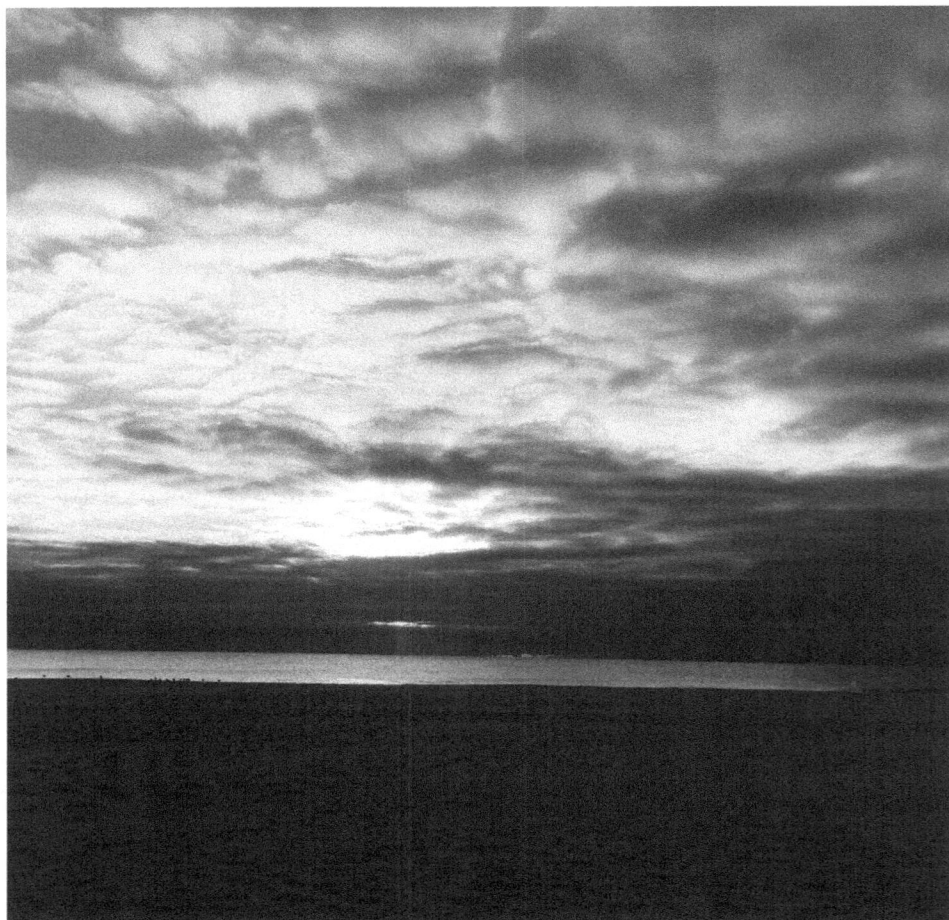

DAY 31
Let your guard down

Go back.

Try again.

One more time.

Luke 5:4-5 When He had stopped speaking, He said to Simon, "Launch out into the deep and let down your nets for a catch." But Simon answered and said to Him, "Master, we have toiled all night and caught nothing; nevertheless at Your word I will let down the net."

The disciples were laboring all night.

And what a long night it must've been. Trying and getting nowhere.

I can hear the discouragement. Disappointment. And exhaustion.

The Lords voice spoke firm, "Go back again."

Is the Lord asking you to try again?

It's hard to launch out into the deep when there are deep hurts. It's hard to trust when trust has been broken. It's hard to love when your love has been rebuffed. It's easier to push away. Go back to shore. Hide. Guard your heart.

It must've seemed like such a waste of time.

Proverbs 14:23 In all labor there is profit.

Nothing you do for the Lord is ever wasted.

He is a Redeemer.

He can restore the years the locust have eaten.

Maybe you're ready to give up on your man, your friend, or even your God.

Go back.

The disciples let down their "nets".

Let your guard down. Be willing to make yourself vulnerable.

God can do a lot with a willing heart. A heart surrendered to the Lord is pliable.

Are you pliable?

Tell Him, "I will."

Simon was trusting the word of Jesus.

Even in the worst case scenario, you can trust His word.

Go with no preconceived notions.

Be willing to forgive. Remember how much your Lord has forgiven you. Don't hold grudges. Let that stuff go. Bitterness and resentment will hold you captive. It will destroy you on the inside. Forgive from the heart. When the Lord calls you to do something, He always gives you the capacity to do it. Just give Him a willing heart.

Father, I will go back and try again. I trust Your word. I do this for You out of obedience. I've been hurt. Help me to be vulnerable again. Here's my heart, Lord. It's Your's. I surrender all the pain. Fill our hearts full to overflowing with love for each other. Restore the trust that's been lost. Redeem what's been lost and restore one hundred fold beyond what we could think possible.

DAY 32
Where are you Lord?

Genesis 22:7 …where is the lamb…?

I hear the boys heart. It's an echo of mine.

Where are you Lord?

Isaac can see things don't look good for him. His very life is being laid on the altar. If God doesn't show up, it's over.

Ever feel like your situation is perfectly hopeless?

Dead.

It's down to the wire.

Is God gonna come through?

Genesis 22:8 And Abraham said, My son, God will provide Himself a lamb for a burnt offering: so they went both of them together.

God sees. He also foresees.

He knows your need.

Matthew 6:8… For your Father knows the things you have need of before you ask Him.

Isaac didn't know the end of the story.

Nor do you.

Our Lord will provide.

Himself.

Only Him.

Are you struggling?

Is God asking something very difficult of you?

In our own human reasoning, we try to figure out how this could possibly work out.

2 Corinthians 10:3-5,7 We are human, but we don't wage war as humans do. We use God's mighty weapons, not worldly weapons, to knock down the strongholds of human reasoning and to destroy false arguments....Do you look at things according to the outward appearance?

Don't look at the outward appearance.

Isaac had no idea what the Lord was doing. There's no hint of panic in his voice. Questions, yes. Panic, no. While Abraham is famous for his faith, Isaac had incredible faith here as well; after all, it was his very life that was at stake. He was readily submitting to the will of his father.

Genesis 22:13 Then Abraham lifted his eyes and looked, and there behind him was a ram caught in a thicket by its horns. So Abraham went and took the ram, and offered it up for a burnt offering instead of his son.

Our great God will provide. He provides in very unexpected ways. Perhaps the ram was already there, and God kept it hidden from their eyes until just the right time.

God always has a ram in the bushes.

Lord God, I rejoice in Your salvation. You are always ahead of me and behind. Help me to keep my eyes looking to You. I confidently expect You to bring me what I need, when I need it and it certainly will be enough. In You I put my hope. Things don't look good right now. You knew we would be in this place and at this time. You're not surprised. You are our Provider. You see all of our need. I know You have a ram in the bushes to meet it. I praise Your Holy Name.

DAY 33
Through the Mountain.

God doesn't always move the mountain..

Just ask Dashrath Manjki. When his wife hurt herself trekking up a rocky footpath, he had to travel around a mountain 43 miles just to get to the nearest hospital.

He decided he needed to do something about this. Not just for his family, but the whole village. They needed access to doctors, schools, and opportunity.

He carved a path through a 300 foot mountain by himself, using only hand tools.

He was just a poor laborer from Gehlour Hills in Bihar, India.

He sold the family's three goats to buy the hammer and chisel and worked every day on the project to make it successful. After plowing fields for others in the morning, he would work on his road all evening and throughout the night.

It took him 22 years.

People called him crazy. Said he'd never be able to do it.

He did it.

Are you facing a mountain?

Matthew 21:21 Then Jesus told them, "I tell you the truth, if you have faith and don't doubt, you can do things like this and much more. You can even say to this mountain, 'May you be lifted up and thrown into the sea,' and it will happen."

Sometimes it's one rock at a time.

James 5:16 ...The effective, fervent prayer of a righteous man avails much.

Prayer is the work.

It is hard work.

When we face adversity and odds and staggering obstacles, common sense says quit.

Faith says persevere. Stay put. Keep going. Don't quit.

Even if you don't see any results, keep praying. Elijah didn't quit. He went back seven times. Finally, the rain came.

Don't have the right tools? I'm just a housewife. Just a grandma. Just a mom. Just a nobody.

God uses nobodies.

1 Corinthians 1:27-28 Instead, God chose things the world considers foolish in order to shame those who think they are wise. And he chose things that are powerless to shame those who are powerful. God chose things despised by the world, things counted as nothing at all, and used them to bring to nothing what the world considers important.

God can use you to make a way where there seems to be no way.

Genesis 18:14 Is anything too hard for the LORD?

Lord Jesus, move this mountain. You know I've tried in my own power. I cannot do it. It must be moved by You and You alone. You are strong enough. Your Power is great. I will continue to seek You. I will not quit. Jesus saturate my marriage with rain from heaven. Water the dry arid places of our souls. Revive us Father.

DAY 34
Suffering, who would choose it?

A gentleman came to visit our homeschool group with some large cages. One cage held old greenery, plants, and caterpillars. Up top there were several chrysalis hanging. Each one was in a different stage of life.

He told us one might give birth that very day, while he was visiting, but I didn't believe it.

Who would ever think they could see a butterfly being born?

Not me that's for sure.

Sure enough it happened. He called us over and I was mesmerized. I couldn't take enough pictures. The birth of a butterfly holds so many metaphors to our marriages. I watched the caterpillar climb up to the top of the cage. She fastened herself to the piece of wood and hung there. Then right before my eyes she turned herself into a letter J. I couldn't help but think of my Jesus. Who willingly walked up the hill carrying His cross. The cross that He would be hung on. He gave his life willingly. No one took it from him. No one forced Him. It was an act of submission to His Father.

He gave his life.

He was then closed in darkness. Buried. In the grave. But God was not through. Jesus Christ was undergoing a metamorphosis.

Maybe today finds you in a place of darkness. Facing adversity. Perhaps you're under pressure and in a very tight place. Is that place in your marriage? A challenging child? Tight financial spot? Illness? Or maybe all of the above?

Luke 22:42 ... "Father, if it is Your will, take this cup away from Me; nevertheless not My will, but Yours, be done."

God didn't take the cup.

He doesn't always remove us from the trial.

He can. He is able.

Sometimes we pray for healing, but God has Resurrection in mind. So much more than we could ever think or imagine.

Hebrews 2:10 For it was fitting for Him, for whom are all things and by whom are all things, in bringing many sons to glory, to make the

captain of their salvation perfect through sufferings.

Suffering is so hard. Who would choose it? Not me nor you. Jesus had to suffer. If our Lord had to suffer why shouldn't we?

Matthew 16:24 Then Jesus said to His disciples, "If anyone desires to come after Me, let him deny himself, and take up his cross, and follow Me."

Our suffering is almost never just for us. Jesus suffered to bring many sons to glory. Our suffering will do the same; it can bring others to Christ. It doesn't seem possible. But, it does.

He gave his life for us. For me. For you. We can never be more like Jesus than laying down our rights. Our will. Our plan.

Philippians 3:10 ...that I may know Him and the power of His resurrection, and the fellowship of His sufferings, being conformed to His death...

We are never more like Jesus than in our suffering. Clothed in darkness, Jesus was not dead. He was about to rise. In this difficult place you find yourself, He is changing you underneath. You need not fear. Don't be afraid to suffer.

Allow Him to do a metamorphosis.

Lord Jesus, I desperately want this change to come about. Change me. I want to become more like You through this dark time. I will keep climbing this difficult hill of suffering. My heart is fastened firmly to Your will. I will not give up. Transform my marriage. Do something radical in my husband's heart. Give him a new heart and mind. Set his heart on fire for Your word like never before. Grant me a new heart and eyes to see my need for it. Make our marriage a display of Your powerful work. There is none like You.

DAY 35
Releasing bitterness

Naomi could not find joy. Who could blame her really? She lost her husband and both of her sons. Her heart was broken. Brokenness can lead to bitterness if we allow it.

Naomi became bitter.

Ruth 1:19 So the two went until they came to Bethlehem. And it came to pass, when they were come to Bethlehem, that all the city was moved about them, and they said, Is this Naomi?

Why didn't they recognize her?

Ruth 1:20 But she said to them, "Do not call me Naomi; call me Mara, for the Almighty has dealt very bitterly with me.

Mara means bitter. And bitter she was. It was written all over her face. Her whole demeanor was changed. She morphed into a person people did not recognize. Her circumstances made her bitter. Don't let that happened to you. Accept where God has you. Don't resent Him. Naomi could never imagine how full her life would become.

Ruth 1:21-22 "I went out full, and the LORD has brought me home again empty. Why do you call me Naomi, since the LORD has testified against me, and the Almighty has afflicted me?" So Naomi returned, and Ruth the Moabitess her daughter-in-law with her, who returned from the country of Moab. Now they came to Bethlehem at the beginning of barley harvest.

Naomi couldn't see this would be the beginning of a harvest in her own life as well. She was too occupied with her circumstances. You can hear her anger.

Psalm 37:8 Cease from anger, and forsake wrath; do not fret—it only causes harm.

Stop being angry! Let it go! Don't hold onto the past; what was said or what was done. Those things will destroy your health. Ruin your marriage.

Philippians 3:13 Brethren, I do not count myself to have apprehended; but one thing I do, forgetting those things which are behind and reaching forward to those things which are ahead.

God desires to take your marriage to a new place. However, it is impossible to get there if you're still holding onto the past. Holding onto the past can literally incapacitate us; making us unable to move, change or be happy.

We can think God is punishing us. He must be really mad at me for "this" to happen.

Condemnation is from the enemy. Let those thoughts go.

Naomi means delight. God delighted in her. He delights in you.

God loves you.

You may desire to let some things go. But, how do you do it?

Abide in the Lord.

Sit with Him and let Him sing over you. When those bitter thoughts come, just worship Him for who He is. He is all things good. Put some worship music on. Sing to Him. Trust in Him.

Naomi didn't recognize that God allowed this. He only has good for us. Nothing happens by chance.

Feed on his faithfulness. Think about how far you have come. What has he brought you through? He has been a steady source of strength. He walked with you. And through it all you became stronger.

Naomi couldn't see the end of the story. God made her full again. Laughter and love overflowed her life.

Death brought life. New and vibrant. God did so much more than she could imagine. He will do the same for you.

Make a decision to bring good out of it.

He gives us the power to forget those things that are behind. To let them go. To forsake wrath. Wrath means to burn. Don't let those things burn inside of you. Take those thoughts and cast them out. Let them go so you can reach forward to the new things that God has for you.

Lord, I acknowledge I don't even know where to begin with putting these things behind me. They are burning inside me. Sometimes I am a person I don't even recognize. I want to move on from here. Wholly remove this root of bitterness before it ruins everything. I lay my past at your feet. Make a beautiful garden out of the ruins. Bring a new and vibrant life to my marriage.

I have a big God

Matthew 17:24-27 On their arrival in Capernaum, the collectors of the Temple tax came to Peter and asked him, "Doesn't your teacher pay the Temple tax?" "Yes, he does," Peter replied. Then he went into the house. But before he had a chance to speak, Jesus asked him, "What do you think, Peter? Do kings tax their own people or the people they have conquered?""They tax the people they have conquered," Peter replied. "Well, then," Jesus said, "the citizens are free! However, we don't want to offend them, so go down to the lake and throw in a line. Open the mouth of the first fish you catch, and you will find a large silver coin. Take it and pay the tax for both of us."

Is Jesus in the details of my life?

I want to share a story with you that will answer this question with a re-sounding, yes. Yes, He is in every single detail of my life and yours.

Does God care about the little things in my life?

Sure, I know He's in the big stuff, but what about the small?

I was scheduled to share with a group of ladies at a Bible study in Cambodia. When I teach, I often like to use tangible items to illustrate the point being made in the verses. In this particular story, I wanted to use silver dollars. I actually had gold dollars in my wallet, but I didn't want gold, I wanted silver. I could've used quarters, but I didn't want to use quarters. I wanted silver dollars. There were only a few days left for me to get these silver dollars when a blizzard struck the Northeast. I was snowed in. It was impossible for me to get to the bank.

What was I going to do?

Not only did I need one silver dollar, according to my list of names, I needed six. One for each woman.

I began talking to the Lord. "Lord you know I need these coins. Well, I don't need them, but I was really depending on them to illustrate the point. What am I going to do?"

And then He brought a thought to my mind. Many years ago, my Aunt Marg collected coins. She had given my granny her collection before she died. About 15 years ago, my granny gave them to me in a small change purse. It is one of the few things that I have that belonged to her. It is very special to me. When I went upstairs, I found that little purse hidden away in my desk.

I opened it up.

Inside was six silver dollars. Exactly what I needed.

Hot tears of joy welled up in my eyes.

I was overwhelmed by the goodness of God.

He is in every detail of my life.

We can see in the above verses, Peter came to Jesus with a need. Jesus anticipated his coming. He was one step ahead of him. Jesus is always one step ahead of us.

What do you need today?

Matthew 6:8 ...your Father knows exactly what you need even before you ask him!

Jesus started meeting my need over 15 years ago. That's amazing. He's preparing things now for my future. He is providing for my children's needs as well. He will meet the needs of my marriage. My finances. All of my personal needs. I want to point out that Peter didn't find a million dollars in the fishes mouth. He found what He needed for that particular day. Jesus will provide what I need for today. He does care about the little things in my life.

Philippians 4:19 And this same God who takes care of me will supply all your needs from his glorious riches, which have been given to us in Christ Jesus.

Father, I am in awe of You. Your sovereign hand has been moving the pieces of my life since Day 1. You've been ordaining circumstances, and arranging all the details to meet this need in my life. My heart. My husband. My marriage. You will supply exactly what I need and when I need it. It will be right on time. I give You glory for what you're going to do. Thank you for caring for the small things as well as the big. I love you Jesus. My King and my God.

DAY 37
Not much hope

I didn't have much hope for her. She was literally just a stick when I planted her. No leaves. Not a branch to be had. Of course, no blossoms.

She really looked dead.

For all intents and purposes she was.

Still, I dug the hole. I put her in it and hoped for the best.

Hope does not disappoint.

She grew slow. At her own pace. In time, she blossomed big. Way more than I expected or dreamed.

So many times our situations can look just like this.

All seems lost. Even hopeless. There is nothing there. And if there is, it isn't anything good. In fact, it may appear to be dying.

God brings beauty out of such pain. Life from dead things. It is a law of God, a seed must die in order to live. It has to be buried before it can come to life.

If you're going through a particularly difficult time right now, wait on the Lord.

He is doing something you can't see.

Just like my rose bush, hidden beneath the soil, God was working. He is making something out of all this adversity.

I get to enjoy the blessing of this flower. Her death and resurrection.

So it will be for you. You will be a comfort to those who have gone through what you're experiencing.

2 Corinthians 1:4 He comforts us in all our troubles so that we can comfort others. When they are troubled, we will be able to give them the same comfort God has given us.

It may not seem so now.

Ezekiel 36:9 See, I care about you, and I will pay attention to you. Your ground will be plowed and your crops planted.

Our heart must be plowed and sown in order to produce fruit for the Kingdom. Just like the soil, it must be broken and cut into in order to produce a garden. While it is painful, it will be worth it.

God can rebuild ruins. He is able to create something out of nothing. Give beauty for ashes.

Ezekiel 36:11 ...I will make you inhabited as in former times, and do better for you than at your beginnings. Then you shall know that I am the LORD.

The best is yet to come. Be patient.

Ephesians 3:20 Now all glory to God, who is able, through his mighty power at work within us, to accomplish infinitely more than we might ask or think.

Jesus Christ, You were the first to rise from the dead. There is nothing in my marriage You cannot raise up. Help me to be patient as You plow the soil of my heart. Break me Lord in those areas You know I need it. Bring a fruitful harvest out of our marriage.

Moses mom put him out there. All alone. Abandoned on the riverbank. Anything could've happened to him. The danger was real. He was in a very precarious position. What would happen to him? Was he going to die? His parents must've been terrified.

Or not.

Hebrews 11:23 By faith Moses, when he was born, was hidden three months by his parents, because they saw he was a beautiful child; and they were not afraid of the king's command.

They emphatically trusted in their God. Perhaps they knew something we need to know.

We are untouchable in the will of God.

His eyes were upon Moses. While Moses seemed to be drifting aimlessly into deep water, God's hand was upon him. At exactly the right time, Pharaohs daughter came along. She drew him out of the water. In fact, that's exactly what the name Moses means. It means "drawn out, picked up, rescued, and saved."

If today finds you in some deep water you can be sure of this, you're not lost.

Your God knows exactly where you are.

He is watching over you. Maybe your marriage is dangerously close to collapse. Your God sees it all. He is taking you somewhere new. Change can be uncomfortable. Maybe its a place you would never go on your own.

Moses was in the hand of God.

From the very beginning, God had a plan.

Every moment of his life was written out.

Revelation 22:13 I am the Alpha and the Omega, the Beginning and the End, the First and the Last."

God knew the end of the story.

Moses would deliver thousands of people out of slavery.

That's a big job. God had to prepare him for that duty.

The preparation took place in the desert. It wasn't quick either.

In the desert God did 4 things:

God humbled him.

God taught him to trust.

God drew him near.

God spoke to him.

When you don't know what tomorrow holds, you can be sure of this:

God holds your tomorrow.

By faith, trust God with your marriage. He is doing something amazing in your life.

Do you trust Him?

Moses was a helpless babe. He couldn't have saved himself if he tried.

God did it all.

He drew him out of that deep water. At precisely the right time. Not a moment too late. Not a moment too early.

He will do the same for you.

Hope in Him. Be still. Know He is God.

God, this could implode at any moment. My eyes are on You. I have absolutely no control over anything. I look to You. Lord Jesus, You are on the throne of my life. Seated. High and lifted up. Nothing moves You. When I am alone, I will trust in You. You are with me. Draw me out of this deep water. I cannot save myself. Save my marriage. I need You Lord.

DAY 39
For His Name

Revelation 2:2-4 "I know your works, your labor, your patience, and that you cannot bear those who are evil. And you have tested those who say they are apostles and are not, and have found them liars; "and you have persevered and have patience, and have labored for My name's sake and have not become weary. "Nevertheless I have this against you, that you have left your first love."

I know.

Two words that mean the world to us when we are struggling and no one knows what we are struggling with. The hidden pain can be overwhelming. It can be physical. And we wonder if anyone knows.

Jesus. He knows.

He knows your works. Your effort. Your endless efforts. What you've done. What you want to do, but can't. Your labor. Pain. Heartache. Your patience. You're remaining under the weight and pressure. In the mix. You can't bear those who do evil.

I know.

You have persevered through all of it. And have patience. John mentions the word "patience" twice in two sentences.

Jesus. He knows your patience.

You have labored for Him. It is His name you're honoring. Everything you do is for Him and His glory. His praise. His reputation.

Jesus. He knows.

You have not become weary. You keep going. Even though you're worn out and worn down.

I know.

Don't quit.

Jesus. He knows.

Don't leave your first love. Jesus is your first love. Your situation, ministry, adversity and pain can cause you to flee away and leave your first love.

159

Jesus. He is the reason. You need to keep maintaining your relationship with Him. You can't let anyone steal that from you.

Revelation 2:17 "He who has an ear, let him hear what the Spirit says to the churches. To him who overcomes I will give some of the hidden manna to eat. And I will give him a white stone, and on the stone a new name written which no one knows except him who receives it."'

If you overcome, you are assured of two things:

Hidden manna. A secret word from the Lord. And a white stone with a new name. A name and a word; only the two of you know. He's the only one who truly knows all the details of your life. Therefore, only He knows what it took for you to keep going. To win the victory.

If you're struggling, Jesus wants to assure your heart, He sees. He cares.

He knows.

He will see you through to the end. He will not leave you.

2 Corinthians 1:18 ...God is faithful...

Lord Jesus, You do know all the longings of my heart. Nothing I have done for you is going unnoticed. Increase my patience under this pressure. I am struggling God. Give me victory. Send me a secret word from heaven. Give me grace to keep persevering. I am determined not to give up.

DAY 40
Parting the sea

Exodus 15:9 The enemy said, 'I will pursue, I will overtake, I will divide the spoil; my desire shall be satisfied on them. I will draw my sword, my hand shall destroy them.'

I can just see the enemy licking his chops.

You know the story well. Pharaoh is pursuing God's people. He has them literally backed up against the wall. No way out. They were doomed.

Things looked impossible.

It can seem like this in our marriage sometimes.

We can feel so frustrated. Like things are never going to change. Finances, prodigal children, step-children, addictions and many other things can bring division into our marriages.

I want you to notice the tactics of the enemy here:

He pursues.

He overtakes.

He divides.

He destroys.

Satan's tactics are the same in our lives.

John 10:10 The thief does not come except to steal, and to kill, and to destroy...

His sole goal is to divide you from your husband.

Your husband is not the enemy.

Ephesians 6:12 For we do not wrestle against flesh and blood, but against principalities, against powers, against the rulers of the darkness of this age, against spiritual hosts of wickedness in the heavenly places.

Your marriage is under attack. If your husband has been taken captive by the enemy, you need to fight for him.

Don't give up on him.

163

Don't distance yourself from him. Draw near to him. Even and especially when you feel like he doesn't deserve it.

Don't dwell on the past. Let those things go.

Let's be humble. Do a lot of overlooking. Forgive and move on.

Exodus 14:21 Then Moses stretched out his hand over the sea; and the LORD caused the sea to go back by a strong east wind all that night, and made the sea into dry land, and the waters were divided.

God made a way when there seemed to be no way.

Let's stretch out our hands to our great God. Ask him to part the sea in our marriages. In those impossible situations. Take the wheels off the enemies chariots. Be a prayer warrior for your husband. If we don't pray for them, who will?

Ecclesiastes 4:12 A person standing alone can be attacked and defeated, but two can stand back-to-back and conquer. Three are even better, for a triple-braided cord is not easily broken.

Father God, we desperately need You to intervene in our marriages. Speak to our husbands. Speak to us. Give us wisdom on when to speak and when to remain silent. Help us to choose encouraging uplifting words that bring life to our marriage. In those areas the enemy is getting the victory, Lord, crush him. Bless our marriages so they will bring honor to Your name. Amen. Amen

DAY 41
Faithful friend

Surrounded. Overwhelmed. Underdog. No way out. Never gonna happen. Outnumbered.

Do you feel like this today?

Psalm 27:3,5 Though an army may encamp against me, my heart shall not fear; though war may rise against me, in this I will be confident...For in the time of trouble He shall hide me in His pavilion; in the secret place of His tabernacle He shall hide me; He shall set me high upon a rock.

Our Lord is a refuge on days like these. His secret place will conceal you and keep you out of reach of the enemy. Completely inaccessible. He will guard and defend against discouragement.

It doesn't necessarily mean your circumstances change.

Your thought life changes.

Is this an hour of distress? Seek His Presence. If earnestly sought, it will not be denied. ~Charles Spurgeon

You and your God, together, you got this.

No one and nothing has ever defeated Him. Not even death. He overcame death. The resurrection is true. He rose from the dead. He is not still dead and inactive. He is working in the midst of you and this situation.

Psalm 27:9 ...You have always been my helper.

Jesus Christ is your faithful friend. To. The. End. He has never wavered. He continues to be with you. Remaining loyal and constant. Even when everyone else abandons, quits and moves on. He'll never desert you.

Psalm 27:6 And now my head shall be lifted up above my enemies all around me; therefore I will offer sacrifices of joy in His tabernacle; I will sing, yes, I will sing praises to the LORD.

This word 'joy' in Hebrew can mean 'blast of war' or 'battle cry'. In our singing and exulting, we can sound the alarm for war. We are at war. The enemy has taken some prisoners. Husbands, children, and loved ones. We can rise up in the face of a great enemy. Declare to the enemy we will not back down. We will fight. And we will get the victory.

Acts 12:5 Peter was therefore kept in prison, but constant prayer was offered to God for him by the church.

It was that constant prayer that won Peter his freedom. Let's sound the alarm. We won't back down. Let's call upon the Lord. He will go to battle for us. He is much stronger, mightier and more powerful than anything we could ever do or say.

Psalm 27:13-14 I would have lost heart, unless I had believed that I would see the goodness of the Lord in the land of the living. Wait on the Lord; be of good courage, and He shall strengthen your heart; wait, I say, on the Lord!

Lord, I am sounding the alarm. Fight for my marriage. You are on my side. Go to battle. You know my husband better than me. You know his struggles and temptations. Strengthen him with might by the power of Your Spirit in his inner man. Help him to win the victory. In his weakness, I will stand in the gap for him. Make our marriage better than it has ever been. Nothing hidden. Everything open before You. Redeem all of the hurt as only You can.

DAY 42
Running through the night

The old guy pulled off one of the most unbelievable feats I've ever heard.

I read about him.

Cliff Young. He ran and ran and ran. Ran for 544 miles. Straight.

Maybe you feel like you're on 544 miles of bad road?

He won an ultramarthon. He was 61 years old and had never even entered a 3 mile race, much less anything more.

His opponents would run for 18 hours and sleep for 6 hours and get up and do the same thing the next day. And the day after. For 6 or 7 days. His strategy was different than everyone else. Cliff ran through the dark. He never stopped. He kept going for 5 straight days. He stunned the crowd. He broke the world record by two whole days.

When it got dark they laid down. Cliff kept going.

Is it dark in your marriage just now?

Don't lie down. Keep going. Endure the hard long stretch. One foot in front of the other.

Do not allow the darkness to extinguish the light inside you. Jesus is your hope.

Now hope does not disappoint.

Keep on loving.

Jesus did.

The darker the night, the brighter the light shines. Odds were staggering that he would win; completely stacked against him. No one thought he could pull this off.

He silenced the naysayers.

Not many would stay if they were you. They would quit.

John 1:5 The light shines in the darkness, and the darkness has not overcome it.

Overcome: katalambano: take hold of, seize possession, obtain what it's after

No darkness can seize possession of your determination.

Father this road seems so long. It is exhausting. Quitting would be so much easier. Fill me with the will to keep going. Keep trying. To love like you love. To give as You gave me. Silence the voice that shouts against all wisdom. I am running for the prize of the upward call you have placed on my life. You are the hope inside me. You have a good plan for me. Plans to prosper me and not harm me. To give me a future and hope. My hope is in You. God you are my rock and strength. Redeem these dark days.

Heavenward

The boy drew it. It was a simple butterfly. But it comes at a time when I need this grace reminder. This prodding to look heavenward. To remember. This life. This pain. It isn't forever. It is temporary. Life is a vapor. And it can change so quickly. When it does, what's a girl to do? Life can become hard overnight. Major decisions to be made. Loved ones fading quickly. Struggling. Sickness is stealing time. Like a bandit. You don't see it coming. You wonder what you could've done differently. What can you do now?

Look up. Heaven is near.

Revelation 21:4 "He will wipe every tear from their eyes, and there will be no more death or sorrow or crying or pain. All these things are gone forever."

Here and now can be painful. So much heartbreak.

A butterfly is made beautiful only through pain.

The struggle is necessary. Darkness a must.

It's in the tight confounds of her cocoon her transformation takes place.

No one can see what's going on underneath. Not even her. She becomes unrecognizable.

Psalm 37:7 Rest in the Lord, and wait patiently for Him...do not fret...

Fretting is like kindling a fire. It will consume you. Every aspect of your thoughts and heart will be destroyed. Your life is in the Lord's hands.

He makes everything beautiful in His time.

If the pressure is mounting, be still. Know He is God. Allow Him to do what He desires.

What emerges from this season of pain, will stun you.

A new creation. Something unimaginable. A whole different you.

Wings. Fluttering wings to soar to new heights.

2 Corinthians 4:17-18 For our present troubles are small and won't last very long. Yet they produce for us a glory that vastly outweighs

them and will last forever! So we don't look at the troubles we can see now; rather, we fix our gaze on things that cannot be seen. For the things we see now will soon be gone, but the things we cannot see will last forever.

These sorrows are temporary.

Fix your eyes on the eternal.

Look beyond the here and now.

As for the butterfly, a life giving fluid must be distributed to her wings in order for her to fly. This can only happen by her vigorous flapping under pressure in a tight dark place.

At just the right time, she emerges. Stunning. Strong. And soaring to new heights.

Heavenward.

Jesus my eyes are on You. The pain of this life is so temporary. Make something beautiful out of all my suffering. Things are hard right now. I can't see what you're doing, but I will trust it is for our good and Your glory. I will be still while You work. Transform my marriage into a magnificent display of Your miracle working power.

DAY 44
Going deeper

The boy wanted hot chocolate.

His rosy cheeks told it was bitter cold outside.

It was a rare morning, we weren't rushed. We lingered at the table long. Me with my hands wrapped tight around my Italian sweet cream coffee. Him with his "hot" chocolate.

His angelic voice spoke soft, "This hot chocolate makes me feel peaceful."

Hot chocolate warms the body, prayer warms the soul.

Prayer brings peace.

Philippians 4:6 Don't worry about anything; instead, pray about everything. Tell God what you need, and thank him for all he has done. Then you will experience God's peace, which exceeds anything we can understand. His peace will guard your hearts and minds as you live in Christ Jesus.

When we tell God what we need, His peace floods our soul. It isn't something that can be explained. His grace permeates our being.

There are depths in the ocean, no storm can touch. There are heights in the sky, where no cloud reaches. Nothing can disturb the serenity.

During the test of a submarine it remained submerged for many hours. When it had returned to the harbor, the commander was asked: "Well, how did the storm affect you last night?" The Commander looked at him in surprise and said: "Storm? We knew nothing of any storm!"

Dwell deep...~Streams in the Valley

Prayer takes us deep into the depths of the heart of God.

It keeps our minds out of the reach of the enemy. His fears. His lies. His doubts cannot touch us.

1 John 4:18 There is no fear in love; but perfect love casts out fear, because fear involves torment. But he who fears has not been made perfect in love.

179

God is love. He loves you. Thank Him for all He's done. He has brought you through some very tough times. He will see you through to the end. He will not leave you. You can trust that He is working all things out for the good of those that love Him and are called according to His purpose.

His purpose and mine look very different sometimes.

Isaiah 55:8-9 "My thoughts are nothing like your thoughts," says the LORD. "And my ways are far beyond anything you could imagine. For just as the heavens are higher than the earth, so my ways are higher than your ways and my thoughts higher than your thoughts."

Thank Him for all He's done. Even for the things you don't understand.

Lord Jesus, thank you for this trial. I know you will use it for good. I acknowledge I don't understand why I've had to go through so much turmoil. Take me deep into the depths of Your love. I need Your peace. Guard me until the storm passes. Keep me settled. I trust Your ways. Save my marriage from the plots and ploys of the enemy. Bless our love.

DAY 45
Jesus never fails

The eviction process is long.

I know firsthand. Friends of ours have a squatter living in their home. He has taken up residence. He won't leave. Outright refuses. He isn't paying the rent. This man has no right to be there. Yet, day after day he occupies their home.

He mocks.

Even taunts.

At times, he even seems to be their friend.

He is not.

He needs to go. Today. Not tomorrow.

Sometimes our thoughts can be just like this squatter.

Don't welcome them in.

Our thoughts are not always our friend.

Thoughts of insecurity, failure, self loathing and defeat; none of these are from the Lord. They have no place in our heart. They tear down. Rob. Kill. Destroy.

Who does that sound like?

The enemy sows tares among the wheat.

Discernment is very important. Line up the thought with the word of God. If it doesn't line up, throw it out.

Evict it. Out you go.

Proverbs 3:5 Trust in the Lord with all your heart, lean not on your own understanding.

When we put our faith in outward circumstances, we give up possession of our joy. Our husbands will disappoint us. They will let us down.

Possession starts with a thought. Just one.

If we don't immediately kick it out, it gains traction. It's in the front door. Before you know it, this thought takes over the whole house.

Possession is seized.

Have some disquieting thoughts entered your mind?

Dismiss them immediately.

Philippians 4:8 ...Fix your thoughts on what is true, and honorable, and right, and pure, and lovely, and admirable. Think about things that are excellent and worthy of praise.

What is true?

You are loved by an amazing God. A God who loves you with an everlasting love. Love that never ever quits. Love that isn't conditional. You are safe. You can feel safe and secure in the Lord. He's holding this all together. He upholds all things by the Power of His word. He has always taken care of you. He will never stop. No matter what happens. You are secure in Him. Your security doesn't lie in another person. What they think or feel about you is irrelevant and trivial. When you aren't sure about anything else, you can be sure of this:

God is faithful.

He will never fail you.

Lord God seize possession of my thought life. Evict these doubts and lies. I believe what Your word says about me. You love me. I am secure in You. Hold my heart. My value lies in You. Your love sustains me. Help my husband to see me as You do. Give him understanding of me. Surround our marriage with Your mighty hand of protection. We give no place for the enemy. Fill our marriage full of Your Spirit of grace. I honor You Lord.

DAY 46
It's Yours Lord

I had a vivid dream last night.

A handful of hope in the midst of pain.

I opened the door to our modest apartment. My husband was directly behind me standing at the stove; his back turned. Just outside the door was a woman walking the biggest dog I'd ever seen. It was all black and looked like a bear. My fear of dogs overwhelmed me. I wasn't about to take any chances of this thing attacking. Without a second thought, I began to slam the door shut.

Before I could get it closed tight, there he was. Fully morphed into a bear, he was quickly overpowering me.

Fighting back, I put everything I had into closing this door.

It was a fierce struggle.

I tried to handle it on my own.

The bear only got bigger. Much bigger than he initially was.

I was no match for this bear.

Realizing I couldn't do this alone, I shouted for my husband to come and help, "There's a bear at the door!"

My man seemed oblivious. Even stirring the pot on the stove. Taking a bite of food. Lackadaisical. I thought to myself, "He doesn't believe me. All of my over exaggerations of past encounters with dogs has tempered his urgency."

Just then I woke up.

I woke up.

There is a bear at the threshold of our doors.

Our marriages, children, ministries, and churches are under attack.

Ecclesiastes 4:9-10 Two are better than one, because they have a good reward for their labor. For if they fall, one will lift up his companion. But woe to him who is alone when he falls, for he has no one to help him up.

Whether you're standing at the stove or standing at the door: it's time to engage.

Push back with all you got.

Ecclesiastes 4:12 Though one may be overpowered by another, two can withstand him. And a threefold cord is not quickly broken.

We have to recognize we can't do this alone.

Psalm 138:3 In the day when I cried out, You answered me, and made me bold with strength in my soul.

We need the Lord. Desperately.

Jeremiah 33:3 'Call to Me, and I will answer you, and show you great and mighty things, which you do not know.'

The battle is the Lord's. And He hasn't lost one yet.

Jesus help us. We need you. You see what no one else sees. We can only see dimly. Teach us to pray. Strengthen us to stand together and fight in prayer for what is Yours. Your marriage. Your children. Your ministry. Your church. Make us bold. Fight for them. We have no power against this great enemy, nor do we know what to do, but our eyes are on You. If You are for us, who can stand against us?

The boy has such a sweet heart.

He extends his hand.

"I don't want any of the squirrels going away empty-handed."

He runs down the trail. Brown leaves crunching under his feet. Cool breeze blowing. Winter is coming. It always does. That squirrel will need to tuck some food away. But right now? He's too busy. Can't be bothered. Or maybe he is bothered by the boy chasing him down. Is he fearful? He could be. Undaunted, the boy follows him into the thick part of the woods.

He got away.

Now the boy is all sad. He expresses his disappointment. I commiserate with him.

I think God understands how he feels.

He doesn't want us going away from Him empty-handed. We do though. When things are going well, we don't need Him so much. Skies are blue and all is well. But, sometimes things aren't so well. We need Him. Winter comes. It always does. Even then, we don't rely on Him. We go off on our own trying to figure things out. Relying on our own intuition instead of seeking our Maker. All the while He pursues after us.

Matthew 11:28 Then Jesus said, "Come to me, all of you who are weary and carry heavy burdens, and I will give you rest."

All we need is found in Him. One word from Him can carry us many days and through deep water. He is extending His hand to you.

His word is food for the soul.

Isaiah 55:11 So is my word that goes out from my mouth: It will not return to me empty, but will accomplish what I desire and achieve the purpose for which I sent it.

Every single thing the world has to offer will leave us empty. God's word fills the void that we can physically feel sometimes. That word or promise He so desperately wants to give you may be for a season to come. A word you will cling to through a cold winter. Or a word to get you through the next hour.

191

Pause for a few moments. Come to Him and take that word He wants to give you. You will not be disappointed.

Father God, I need You. Right now I am asking You to speak to my heart. Write a message in the depths of my soul to sustain me through this season. I am hungry for you. As I slow down, meet with me. Let's sit together. I want to hear Your heart. Tell me Your heart for my husband. How do You feel about him? Show me how to love him as You do. Fill me full Lord. I don't want to go away empty-handed.

DAY 48
Waiting for the impossible

The sun is just beginning to peek through.

I hear a lovely melody. Exuberant and joyful.

It's the birds singing their song.

They don't know what today holds. Where will they get there food? Who will provide for them?

These girls aren't thinking about that. They have no cares. They're not worried.

They're singing their hearts out.

Matthew 6:26 "Look at the birds of the air, for they neither sow nor reap nor gather into barns; yet your heavenly Father feeds them. Are you not of more value than they?"

They are content.

1 Timothy 6:6 Now godliness with contentment is great gain.

Their song exudes confidence.

Psalm 27:3 Though an army encamp against me, my heart shall not fear; though war arise against me, yet I will be confident.

We do not have to fear what today holds.

Our God is holding our today in the palm of His hand. We are secure in Him.

Psalm 62:1 To the Chief Musician. To Jeduthun. A Psalm of David. Truly my soul silently waits for God; from Him comes my salvation.

This was written to the leader of songs, Jeduthun. His name means praising. No matter what you're facing, you can put your praise on. Sing your heart out to the Lord. He is working all things out for your good.

Psalm 37:5 Commit your way to the LORD, trust also in Him, and He shall bring it to pass.

"When God is doing something wonderful, He begins with a difficulty. If it's going to be something very wonderful, He begins with an impossibility."~Charles Inwood

That is exactly what happened in Abraham's life.

The Lord told him he would have a son.

Genesis 15:6 And Abram believed the Lord, and the Lord counted him as righteous because of his faith.

That son didn't come until he was one hundred years old.

Utterly impossible.

Abraham believed the word of the Lord. And you can too.

The Lord allows us to go through these dark nights so the whole world can know it was Him that brought us through. Take some time to sing to Him. It honors Him when we trust in those areas we can't see. You need not fear. He provided for Abraham. He will provide for you through the dark nights. Sing your song. The sun will be peeking through before you know it.

Lord Jesus I commit my marriage to you. I will not be consumed by worries. Instead, I will worship You with all my heart. Lead me to Your throne of amazing grace. Your faithfulness stretches to the sky. You will take care of me. This I know. Power belongs to You O God. My soul will wait quietly for You.

DAY 49
My secret

This is big. Real big. Of the utmost importance. Hear it loud and large.

Our Lord has given us a secret weapon to combat the enemy:

Making love with your husband.

Genesis 2:24 Therefore a man shall leave his father and mother and be joined to his wife, and they shall become one flesh.

This word "joined" is the Hebrew word "dabaq." It quite literally means "to glue."

Sex is the super-glue of your marriage.

It is a great mystery. One I do not fully understand. However, I trust.

There have been times my husband and I seem so far apart. It's embarrassing. The Pastor and his wife can't seem to get it together. Sex closes that gap.

The two become one.

Other times, we are throwing swords at each other. Fears run rampant. Sex knits our hearts together. Again.

The two become one.

We get angry at each other. Walls go up. High walls. Sex breaks down the walls.

The two become one.

I received some real wise advice from my Pastor's wife before I got married. I will pass it on:

Never tell your husband "No."

In 15 years, I may have rebuffed him twice. It was in rare circumstances.

Now, have there been times I wanted to say, "No?" More times than I can count.

Your husband needs you.

He needs you to want him. To know you are attracted to him.

Flirt with him. Send him a suggestive text. Write him a love note.

Show him you think he's a hottie.

Grab some new lingerie in his favorite color and material. Lacy? Silky?

The two shall become one. Be "joined" to your husband.

Use that super-glue. Often.

Your husband will be one happy camper.

Ephesians 5:31-32 "For this reason a man shall leave his father and mother and be joined to his wife, and the two shall become one flesh." This is a great mystery, but I speak concerning Christ and the church.

Father Lord, giver and Creator of love, do more than I could ever ask or imagine in our bed. I want to give myself freely and unreservedly to my husband. Let my touch thrill him. Turn the tables on the enemy as we give ourselves to each other. Make us one, like only You can.

Sitting at His feet

I can't blame her much. Martha that is.

She was feeling overwhelmed.

A girl can get engulfed sometimes.

All the needs before her. That's all she can see.

Yeah, I'm there all the time.

How am I going to get all this done? Will we ever get there? What will happen when…?

Where? Who? Why? All the expectations. And all the doubts. What if's….

Jesus spoke gentle words.

Luke 10:41… "My dear Martha, you are worried and upset over all these details."

This word "upset" gives us a great picture in the Latin root. It means a crowd or a riotous multitude. All of these things that we see before us, the needs, the lack, the unanswered questions, the exhaustion of service, the distance, the doubts; all of these things can crowd out what is most important.

Luke 10:42 "There is only one thing worth being concerned about. Mary has discovered it, and it will not be taken away from her."

Only one thing was needed.

Mary discovered it.

Luke 10:39 Her sister, Mary, sat at the Lord's feet, listening to what He taught.

I forget. This is Your marriage. These are Your people. This man belongs to You. I don't have to have all the answers.

Are you feeling overwhelmed?

Sit at Jesus feet.

As you go about your day, talk to Him. Walk with Him. Ask Him for wisdom.

James 1:5 If you need wisdom, ask our generous God, and he will give it to you.

Don't speak unless you know He wants you to speak.

James 1:19 Understand this, my dear brothers and sisters: You must all be quick to listen, slow to speak, and slow to get angry.

Jesus is in the particulars. Every last one. He will provide for all of your needs.

Philippians 4:19 And this same God who takes care of me will supply all your needs from his glorious riches, which have been given to us in Christ Jesus.

Jesus I will come and sit at Your feet. There is no other place I need to be today. Everything else can wait. I need You. Give me wisdom. I'm just not sure where to go next. What should I say, if anything at all? Take away this distance; bridge the gap. Dispel the tensions. Ease my burdens. You know what we need. I trust You will provide.

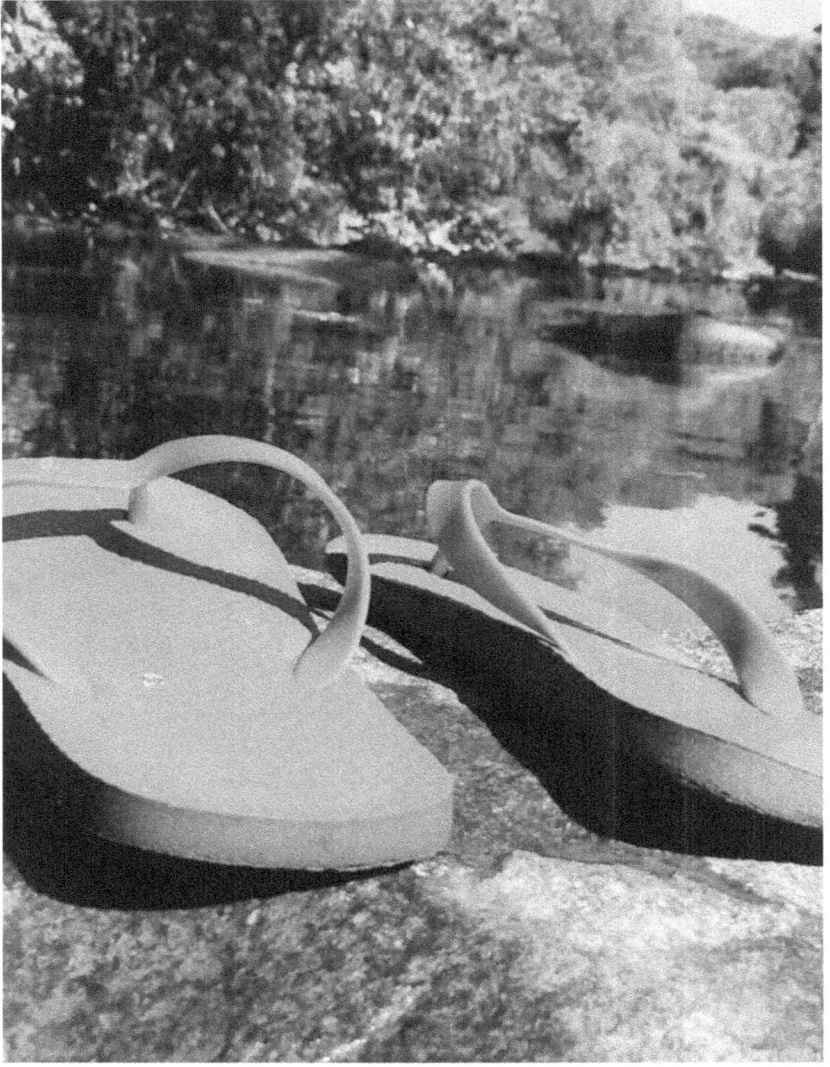

DAY 51
Stepping out

I watched close.

The boy tread light. He walked as far as he could on the rocky shore. He wanted to explore some new territory. Go out farther and deeper.

Wanting to try this new adventure, he took the first step.

He could've stayed on the shore. He didn't.

He waded into unknown waters.

It was murky, one couldn't see the bottom.

Going slow was key.

Unsteady terrain; large rocks covered with moss make a slippery slope. Feet may fail.

He stayed the course. He didn't let his fears get the best of him. Nor the fact that he didn't have his bathing suit on. Just some ordinary shorts.

This was a big deal to him. Maybe not so much to anyone else, but for him this was exciting.

He was filled with confidence. His smile spoke what was in his heart.

"I can do this."

Where did his confidence come from?

His Dad was right there. Never took his eyes off of him. Not even for a second.

As he waded deeper, Dad went right behind. Hand stretched out. Just in case he needed some support. Dad ensured his safety. There was no need to fear.

Dad was right behind him.

Are you in murky waters?

Joshua was. He knew what it was like to be facing the unknown.

The Lord spoke clear.

Joshua 1:5 No one will be able to stand against you as long as you live. For I will be with you as I was with Moses. I will not fail you or abandon you.

Joshua would face war. And giants. And fear. And discouragement.

Through it all, the Lord was with him. He is with you too.

Philippians 4:13 I can do all things through Christ who strengthens me.

He will never leave you. You may not be able to see how this is all going to work out.

God sees it all.

Revelation 1:8 "I am the Alpha and the Omega, the Beginning and the End," says the Lord, "who is and who was and who is to come, the Almighty."

God sees the beginning. He sees the end. He sees everything in between.

Every specific. He is in the middle of this. He will provide.

He always has and He always will. In His own way. In His own time.

Father God, I remember what You've done in the past. You gave me more than enough to accomplish Your will. I am afraid. Even so, I will keep walking in Your will. You are the God of my strength. Fill me with courage. Preserve my life from fear of the enemy. Your steadfast love will surround me with deliverance. Walk through this with me.

DAY 52
Abundant supply

Mark 8:1 About this time another large crowd had gathered, and the people ran out of food again.

The disciples saw the need before them and they were overwhelmed.

The demands. Surely there was crying. And complaining. Finger pointing. And fighting.

They were tired. Here they were again in the same exhausting circumstance.

Lots of people. A whole lot of needs.

I have a child at home. I can feel like that. Maybe you have six. Or two with very strong wills. Or one with special needs. You can barely meet their physical needs, much less do anything else. Or maybe you have none. That need deep inside can be just as difficult. Or you may face a multitude of marital issues. In any case, there is a great need.

Mark 8:4 His disciples replied, "How are we supposed to find enough food to feed them out here in the wilderness?"

They were looking at their circumstances, and wondering how in the world they were going to feed all these people. They didn't have enough. It can feel like that in marriage sometimes. We can barely keep up. Throw some tension in there, and life gets overwhelming quick.

When the disciples saw the multitude, they concluded it was their job to feed them. They were wrong. Their eyes were on the wrong thing.

It was Jesus job. These were His people.

He would provide for them.

He will provide for you and your spouse.

Philippians 4:19 And my God shall supply all your need according to His riches in glory by Christ Jesus.

Whatever your need, Jesus will fill it. Keep your eyes on Him.

Mark 8:5 Jesus asked, "How much bread do you have?"

That day they had seven loaves. They offered it willingly from the heart.

Jesus multiplied it. He ended up feeding 4,000 men that day.

In His hands, it became enough.

What do you have?

You may have nothing. Offer your heart. Your willingness to please Him.

Place it in His hands. Don't focus on what is lacking.

Give thanks. You will have enough. More than enough.

Jesus has a way of making sure of it.

Lord Jesus, I remember what you've done in the past. You met my need in abundance. In this barren season, give me the power to remain steadfast to my husband. I only have a little bit to give. Would you multiply it and make it enough; with some left over? Only You can satisfy the deep longings of my heart. Pour out Your blessings on my marriage. I open my heart and give you what I have in full surrender.

Unruffled and resting

Matthew 8:24...But Jesus was sleeping.

Oh so calm. Unruffled. Resting well.

The disciples? They were freaking out. A fierce storm had come upon them. Waves were covering the boat. Wind was whipping. They just knew death was imminent. Surely they would drown.

Ever feel like that?

You're praying and things are going from bad to worse. It is serious. If things don't change, something real bad is gonna go down. You're desperate. And anxiety and worry start to overtake all your thoughts. Things intensify. You just need help.

Where is Jesus?

He was right there in the boat with the disciples. Here was the problem: they took their eyes off Jesus. They put their eyes on the waves. That overwhelmed them. They could feel the wind. It scared them. Our feelings can deceive us. We tend to assume the worse.

Matthew 8:26 Jesus responded, "Why are you afraid? You have so little faith!" Then he got up and rebuked the wind and waves, and suddenly there was a great calm.

Jesus is in the boat. Still. He hasn't left you.

Proverbs 3:5 Trust in and rely confidently on the Lord with all your heart and do not rely on your own insight or understanding.

We can't rely on what our outward circumstances look like.

Hebrews 11:1 Now faith is the assurance of things hoped for, and the evidence of things not seen.

Faith confirms the things we hope for that are divinely guaranteed, and it is evidence of what we cannot see. Faith comprehends as fact what cannot be experienced by our physical senses.

We can trust in Jesus to work in our situation. At just the right time. He is always on time.

He is never too early. And surely, He is never too late.

Habakkuk 2:3 …though it tarries, wait for it; it will surely come.

Jesus, author of marriage, You are in mine. I see the waves. They are crashing in on me. You see me. You know my fearful heart. Rebuke the wind. Bring a calm to these raging waters. Speak to my heart. Breathe Your peace upon my mind. Quiet my rambling thoughts. Get us safely to our destination. Increase my faith to trust you more than I ever have before.

Psalm 23:1 The Lord is my shepherd

So much wrapped up in one little word:

Shepherd.

A shepherd leads his sheep. He leads them away from harmful things. Things that would not be good for them. Sheep are notoriously stupid. Wandering off. Getting into things that may hurt them. Or make them sick. And get them in trouble.

Sheep don't know what's best for them.

They think they do. That's why they need a shepherd. The shepherd will lead them the best way. Not necessarily the easiest way. He'll lead them gently. With tender care. And soft touch. If they wander off, he goes to get them. If he has one hundred sheep, he will leave the 99 to go searching for the one.

When the shepherd leads them up a difficult path, he goes slow. He walks each step with them.

Sheep have everything they need. The shepherd makes sure if it. They can depend on him. There's no need to fear. He will provide for them.

Sheep have a flocking instinct. They need each other. A sheep lagging behind or isolating itself is an indication that it's sick.

They band together for protection. There is safety in numbers. It is harder for a predator to pick off a sheep out of a group than to go after a stray.

Is your marriage on a rocky path? Strenuous terrain? Is it dark? Don't separate yourself.

You can trust the Shepherd.

He is taking you somewhere good. It may not seem good at the moment, but it is necessary. Everything God does has purpose.

God wastes nothing.

Are you completely stressed out?

Follow the Shepherd. He is leading you to waters of rest. Tranquil. And still. Even though you don't know what lies over the next hill. Rest. If and when you're in the darkest valley. Rest. Especially if predators are lurking. Rest.

He restores your soul. Renewing your strength to do what He called you to do. Spend some time in the waters of His word. It will breathe life into your spirit. Refreshing and reviving you.

Rest.

Your shepherd will never leave you.

He is with you. To the end.

Lord, my great Shepherd, I am afraid. I am worn out. Lead me to your quiet waters of rest. Give me tranquillity in my spirit. You lead, I will follow. Your way is the best way. It may not be the easiest, but I trust it's the best. I will not isolate myself. Draw me near to the heart of my husband. Restore the love and laughter we once shared. Empty us of pride and fill us with humility. Overwhelm us with your Holy Spirit.

Wanting out; staying in

I just want out.

This is more than I can endure.

That's certainly how I would've felt.

John was in a rocky, barren, sweltering hot place. A place of discomfort.

Dry. Longing for a respite of any kind.

None coming.

John was banished to the Isle of Patmos. Rome sent its prisoners there to live out their sentence. Alone.

Feeling alone can be a sentence all its own.

Something extraordinary happens in John's aloneness.

He ends up getting the most incredible revelation of Jesus Christ known to man. Patmos means "my killing." Pretty sure I've been there a few times. This place is going "to kill me."

3 things happen on this island called Patmos:

1. God shows up.

God had him there for a reason. God gave him a message he couldn't receive in any other place. There are times God just needs to get us alone. He often uses our circumstances to do that.

2. God comforts him.

Revelation 1:17 And when I saw Him, I fell at His feet as dead. But He laid His right hand on me, saying to me, "Do not be afraid; I am the First and the Last."

When we're prisoners of our circumstances, God comes and lays His hand upon us. He reassures us in our fear. He knows exactly where we are. He hasn't forgotten us. We're not out of His sight.

3. God puts a call on his life.

John had a new assignment.

Revelation 1:19 "Write the things which you have seen, and the things which are, and the things which will take place after this.".

God engraved a message on his heart that is still speaking.

Are you on "the isle of Patmos" today? Is your marriage in a rocky barren place? Ask God: "What do You want to say to me?"

Nothing happens by accident. He has a purpose for everything.

Give Him time to speak.

Psalm 46:10 Be still and know that I am God.

Dear Lord, I just want out of this. Help me to realize I cannot depend on my feelings. Forgive me for wanting to give up sometimes. Make me wise to the enemies crafty persuasions. Cast him behind my back. As he tries to lure me away from my holy time with You, I will press on. Determined. Not persuaded. Not drawn away. But nearer to You my Jesus. Fill me with Your Holy Spirit. Even when I can't feel You close, I will trust You are. You know exactly where I am at all times. I am not alone.

DAY 56
Death brings life

John 19:41 Now in the place where He was crucified there was a garden, and in the garden a new tomb in which no one had yet been laid.

A garden in the most unlikely place. Surrounded by death. Anguish. And pain.

Something beautiful in the midst.

One of the greatest paradoxes in the Bible:

Death brings life.

Matthew 16:24 Then Jesus said to His disciples, "If anyone desires to come after Me, let him deny himself, and take up his cross, and follow Me.

Every time you pick up your cross, you have to put something down.

Your desires. Your will. Your pride. Your rights.

1 John 3:16 By this we know love, because He laid down His life for us. And we also ought to lay down our lives for the brethren.

Love lays down. Backs down. Stands down.

Matthew 16:25 "For whoever desires to save his life will lose it, but whoever loses his life for My sake will find it."

A cross and nails. That is love. Death and humility and pain.

Love draws near even when rejected. And the only thing you want to do is pull away. Drive away. And never look back. Loves draws nearer just then.

The cross looked like the biggest tragedy. And it would've been. But that was not the end of the story.

The resurrection happened. Jesus didn't stay dead. He is alive!

Turned out to be the biggest life giving victory in history.

His story. It can be your story.

Is there a place you can choose to lay down? Be buried? Give?

God gave. Even when it hurt.

John 3:16 "For God so loved the world that He gave His only begotten Son, that whoever believes in Him should not perish but have everlasting life."

Now fill in the blank with your name:

For God so loved_____that He gave His only begotten Son...

He didn't die just for good people. People who deserved it. He died for bad people. Those who didn't deserve it. Like me. He laid down His life so I could live forever in heaven with Him. He paid the penalty I justly deserved. Life from His death is mine.

That is a beautiful thing.

Lord Jesus, Your name is love. Your way is love. I will follow You. I choose to pick up my cross and love this man. Love will have the victory today. Raise these dead places in my marriage back to life. Revive them from the grip of sin and death and the grave. You are alive and living in me. You are greater than he that is in the world. He that is trying to overcome me with his lies. I purpose to defeat the enemy by loving my husband. Destroy the works of the enemy. That is why you came. Nothing in our marriage is beyond your Redeeming love.

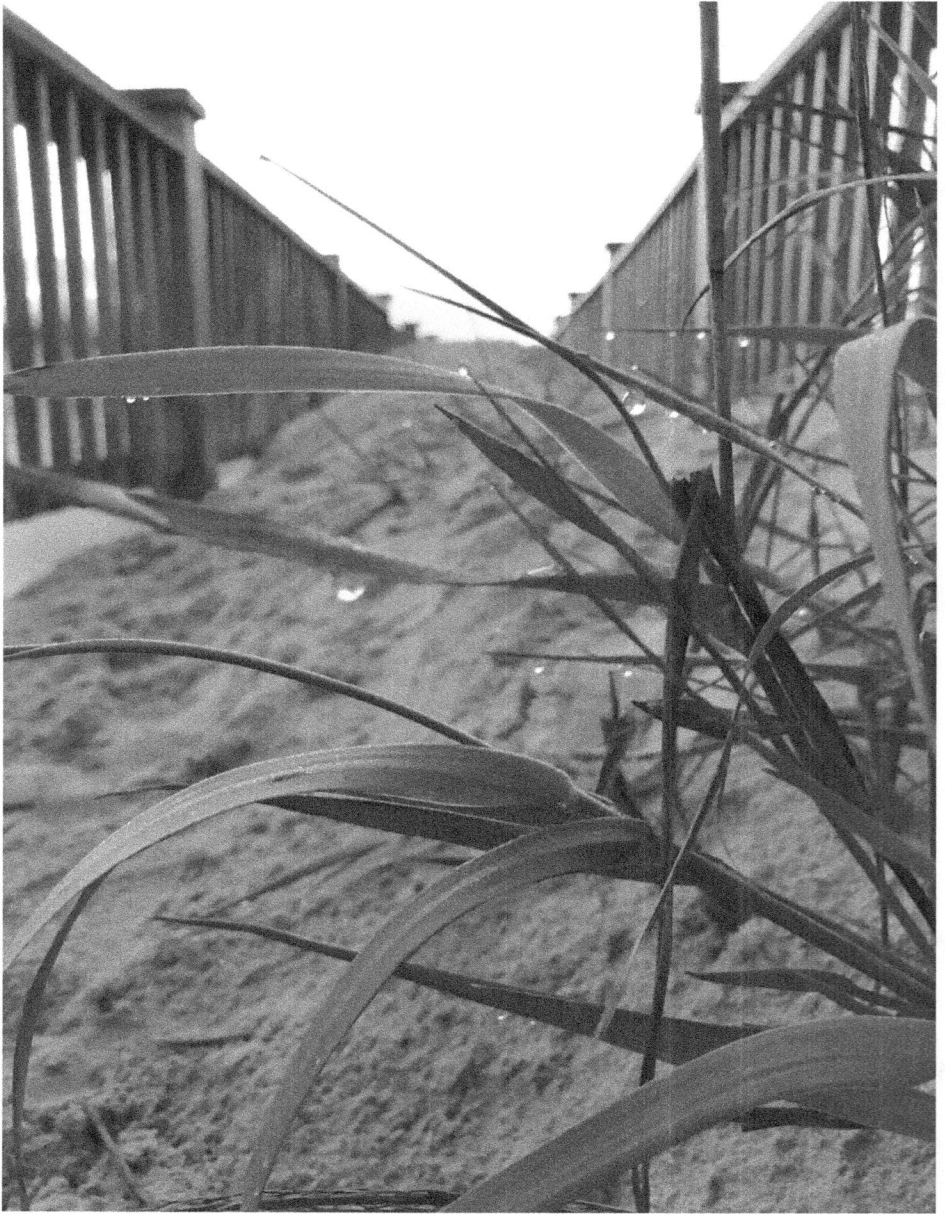

DAY 57
Yes!

Exodus 16:4 Then the LORD said to Moses, "Behold, I will rain bread from heaven for you. And the people shall go out and gather a certain quota every day, that I may test them, whether they will walk in My law or not.

Day in and day out.

One day at a time.

That's how God provided.

It's still that way for us.

We need a fresh "quota" everyday.

This word "quota" is interesting. It's the Hebrew word "dabar." It's used in various other places to mean: a word, a promise, a message or a song.

Each day God has a message for us from His word. Sent straight from His heart.

It's our responsibility to go get it.

Yes, that takes effort. It really takes planning.

For us, it may mean saying "no" to a lot of good things.

Wives who say, "Yes" to God will be filled with new strength every single day.

Don't we need to be filled up daily? The world zaps everything out of us. A wife can be overcome quickly. We are made to love and be loved by our Creator. What He provides cannot be found anywhere else.

Exodus 16:21 So they gathered it every morning, every man according to his need. And when the sun became hot, it melted.

Each day, when the sun became hot, the manna melted.

Why?

They needed to depend on Jesus every day. He showed them they could do nothing without Him.

We need Jesus. He made us that way. He wants us to seek Him. That's how relationships are built. Daily time spent together. Talking. Sharing life. Listening. And being heard.

Shooting off a text is NOT a relationship.

A cursory nod. A few words scattered to the wind. That will never do.

God has a message for you.

Every. Single. Day. Go get it.

It will be life for your soul.

He promises to meet us right where we're at.

When we seek Him, we will find Him.

Jeremiah 29:13 And you will seek Me and find Me, when you search for Me with all your heart.

Lord God, I am hungry for You. Satisfy the deepest longings of my soul. Those places that hurt. That no one sees. No one knows. You know. Here I am Lord. Desperate for a word from You. I won't make it this day without it. I will slow way down. Tarry with You. Await You. Expect You. Meet my husband where he's at. Only You can know what he needs to hear. Speak to him Lord.

DAY 58
Nevertheless

2 Samuel 5:6-7 And the king and his men went to Jerusalem against the Jebusites, the inhabitants of the land, who spoke to David, saying, "You shall not come in here; but the blind and the lame will repel you," thinking, "David cannot come in here."Nevertheless David took the stronghold of Zion (that is, the City of David).

You can't. You won't. You'll never be able to do that. Hearing all that? A guy could get real discouraged.

I LOVE this word: **Nevertheless**.

Nevertheless David took the stronghold.

He did what they said he could never do.

David took possession of what was in the enemies hands.

He seized ownership. Took back what was rightfully his.

Check out what happened next:

2 Samuel 5:9 Then David dwelt in the stronghold, and called it the City of David. And David built all around from the Millo and inward.

David made this place his home.

This "Millo" in the Hebrew literally means landfill or trash heap.

David built something great right on top of that pile of trash.

That big mess became something beautiful.

Do you have any really big messes in your life right about now?

You see, what God did in David's life, He can do in yours.

David went on and became great. The Lord was with Him.

The Lord is with you. It may not feel like it.

Nevertheless.

Maybe you're assessing your situation by what others have to say or think. Or perhaps you are overcome with fear. You wonder, what is the use? This is all a big waste.

God wastes nothing.

When we look at the outward circumstances, it does look awful.

Even impossible.

Luke 1:37 For nothing is impossible with God.

He can do anything. He did create the world in 6 days.

God builds and He rebuilds on top of old ruined landfills.

You keep persevering. Cling to the promise of God. His word will never fail.

Ephesians 6:10 Finally, my brethren, be strong in the Lord and in the power of His might.

God, silence the continual mocking voice in my life. Whispering lies. Block it out. Father, I want to do what David did. With You I know I can. I am able because You are able. You are strong. I am weak. I cannot overcome the enemy on my own. On my own, I make a mess. There seem to be a lot of messes in my marriage. Help me to persevere through all of it. Rebuild something more beautiful than I can imagine on the ruined places. Breathe life into the heart of our relationship. Make it vibrant and joyful. Until You do, I will cling to Your promise.

DAY 59
Keep knocking

I meet this kid. His words captivate me.

As he looks down, he speaks soft.

"My Dad says when God doesn't answer my prayers it's because He's too busy for me."

I feel my heart break.

God is never too busy for his children. Never.

He doesn't always answer right away. He does always answer.

Sometimes we need to keep going back to Him. Asking. Knocking.

Sometimes outright begging.

It is not because He is too busy.

He is working. Wanting you and everyone around you to know He is God.

He and He alone can do miracles. He changes times and seasons. Opens the eyes of the blind. Lifts the veil from the deceived. Redeems.

Only He can do the impossible. He is the One true God.

He uses our circumstances to prove it.

God did just that with the false prophets of Baal.

Elijah called all 450 of them together. He tells them to bring two bulls. Choose whichever one they wish and cut it into pieces and lay it on the wood of their altar, but without setting fire to it. He prepared a bull and did the same. Then he challenged them to call on their god to answer by setting fire to the wood. He would do the same. The God who answered by setting fire to the wood was the true God. Elijah had them go first. They prepared one of the bulls and placed it on the altar. Then, they called on their false god from morning until noontime.

Nothing. No reply of any kind.

Elijah began mocking them. "Shout louder. Is your god away on a trip, or is he sleeping?"

They raved all afternoon. Shouting. Still nothing. No reply. No response.

Elijah called to the people. They gathered. He repaired the altar of the Lord that was torn down. He took twelve stones to rebuild the altar in the name of the Lord. Then he dug a trench around the altar large enough to hold about three gallons of water. He piled wood on the altar, cut the bull in pieces, and laid the pieces on the wood.

Then he had them fill four large jars with water, and pour the water over the offering and the wood. After that, he had them do it again. And then, a third time. The water ran around the altar and even filled the trench.

Pouring water and more water on the sacrifice made the task exceptionally difficult.

Sometimes our situations have to get worse before they get better.

Elijah walked up to the altar and prayed for God to prove He was God. He wanted the people to know He is Lord and that He had brought them back to Himself.

Immediately the fire of the Lord flashed down from heaven and burned up the young bull, the wood, the stones, and even the dust. It consumed all the water too!

Psalm 86:8 Among the gods there is none like You, O Lord; nor are there any works like Your works.

God is setting Himself apart. He is showing us Who He is!

Lord Jesus, there is nothing too hard for you. You are the God of the impossible. I will not look to the ways of the world for my help. My eyes are on You. You will never disappoint me. Prove how powerful You are to all who look at my life. May Your name be honored. You are Sovereign. Almighty. Strong. Courageous. My strong tower. Refuge. Show the world who You are through my marriage. Do the impossible.

DAY 60
Loving Father

I watched her close.

She went straight to the light.

Fluttering and flitting. Coming close. But, backing away. Again and again. Always coming to the light. While the darkness seemed so much bigger, and wider, and vast, she came to the light.

She chose well.

Each of us have a similar choice to make. A big decision. It is not one to take lightly.

What we choose here and now, will greatly effect our eternity.

Each one of us will live forever. That is a guarantee. You have the power to choose where you will spend eternity. Choose well. Choose now. There will be a time, no one knows when that is, that God will remove the Holy Spirit. Thus, allowing a strong delusion on those who reject Him.

2 Thessalonians 2:9-12 The coming of the lawless one is according to the working of Satan, with all power, signs, and lying wonders, and with all unrighteous deception among those who perish, because they did not receive the love of the truth, that they might be saved. And for this reason God will send them strong delusion, that they should believe the lie, that they all may be condemned who did not believe the truth but had pleasure in unrighteousness.

This verse literally took my breath away this morning. The word "condemned" is translated "damned." People are damned to hell.

What people?

People who do not believe the truth. People who had pleasure in unrighteousness.

John 3:19 "And this is the condemnation, that the light has come into the world, and men loved darkness rather than light, because their deeds were evil."

Who is the light?

John 8:12 NKJV Then Jesus spoke to them again, saying, "I am the light of the world. He who follows Me shall not walk in darkness, but have the light of life."

Jesus is the light. Are you walking in the light? Is your husband?

Eternity is at stake.

Would a loving God send someone to hell?

Absolutely not!

Jesus Christ is a loving Father. And just like any loving Father, He gives his children a choice. He didn't make us robots. We get to choose to follow and obey Him. People who choose to do whatever they want and live as they please with a full understanding of what is right, have made a conscience choice to turn their back on God. Essentially choosing hell.

Please hear the heart of our loving Father pleading with you to come to Him. Coming to Him means walking away from your life of sin.

Matthew 4:17 From then on Jesus began to preach, "Repent of your sins and turn to God, for the Kingdom of Heaven is near."

Repent simply means to change your mind. In other words, I was going east and Jesus was going west. I'm gonna stop going east and head in His direction. As soon as you make that choice, Jesus will run to meet you. Ask Him to forgive you. It doesn't matter what you've done in the past. All of that will be washed away the moment you confess. Give Him your heart and He'll change your life. He will fill you with the Holy Spirit. His Spirit will give you the power to overcome temptation and live for Him.

Jesus loves you. How do you know that?

John 3:16 "For God loved the world so much that he gave his one and only Son, so that everyone who believes in him will not perish but have eternal life."

You are loved. Your life has value. Jesus doesn't look at your past. He looks at what you will become. What will you become?

The sky is the limit!

1 Corinthians 2:9 That is what the Scriptures mean when they say, "No eye has seen, no ear has heard, and no mind has imagined what God has prepared for those who love him."

Father, give my husband understanding of how much you love him. Open my own eyes wide to Your love. Your love is enough. Send Your Holy Spirit of conviction where there is even a hint of compromise. Help us surrender fully to You in every area. Our marriage is a picture of You and the church. I want our marriage to be a display of Your love. I recognize eternity is on the line. Lord, may many come to know You through our marriage union.